THE INCOMPETENT DOCTOR

STATE OF HEALTH SERIES

Edited by Chris Ham, Director of Health Services Management Centre, University of Birmingham

THE INCOMPETENT DOCTOR

Behind Closed Doors

Marilynn M. Rosenthal

Open University Press
Buckingham · Philadelphia

Open University Press
Celtic Court
22 Ballmoor
Buckingham
MK18 1XW

and
1900 Frost Road, Suite 101
Bristol, PA 19007, USA

First Published 1995

A catalogue record of this book is available from the British Library

Library of Congress Cataloging-in-Publication Data
Rosenthal, Marilynn M.
    The incompetent doctor: behind closed doors/Marilynn M.
    Rosenthal
        p.   cm. — (State of health series)
    Includes bibliographical references and index.
    ISBN 0–335–19109–6 (pbk.)   ISBN 0–335–19110–X (hb)
    1. Medical care—Quality control. 2. Peer review. 3. Clinical
competence. 4. Physicians—Discipline. 5. Medical errors. 6. Problem
employees. 7. Social control. 8. National Health Service (Great Britain)
I. Series.
    [DNLM: 1. Clinical Competence. 2. Peer Review. Health Care. 3.
Malpractice—Great Britain. W 21 R8151 1995)
    RA399.A1R67   1995
    362.1'72'0685—dc20
DNLM/DLC
for Library of Congress   94–36859
                                                                      CIP

Typeset by Type Study, Scarborough
Printed in Great Britain by St Edmundsbury Press,
Bury St Edmunds, Suffolk

This book is dedicated to my son and good friend, Joshua Alan Rosenthal. Intelligent, caring, assertive, humorous; a delightful conversationalist and a sympathetic listener. With love, thanks, understanding.

CONTENTS

SERIES EDITOR'S INTRODUCTION

Health services in many developed countries have come under critical scrutiny in recent years. In part this is because of increasing expenditure, much of it funded from public sources, and the pressure this has put on governments seeking to control public spending. Also important has been the perception that resources allocated to health services are not always deployed in an optimal fashion. Thus at a time when the scope for increasing expenditure is extremely limited, there is a need to search for ways of using existing budgets more efficiently. A further concern has been the desire to ensure access to health care of various groups on an equitable basis. In some countries this has been linked to a wish to enhance patient choice and to make service providers more responsive to patients as 'consumers'.

Underlying these specific concerns are a number of more fundamental developments which have a significant bearing on the performance of health services. Three are worth highlighting. First, there are demographic changes, including the ageing population and the decline in the proportion of the population of working age. These changes will both increase the demand for health care and at the same time limit the ability of health services to respond to this demand.

Second, advances in medical science will also give rise to new demands within the health services. These advances cover a range of possibilities, including innovations in surgery, drug therapy, screening and diagnosis. The pace of innovation is likely to quicken as the end of the century approaches, with significant implications for the funding and provision of services.

Third, public expectations of health services are rising as those who use services demand higher standards of care. In part, this is stimulated by developments within the health service, including the availability of new technology. More fundamentally, it stems from the emergence of a more educated and informed population, in which people are accustomed to being treated as consumers rather than patients.

Against this background, policymakers in a number of countries are reviewing the future of health services. Those countries which have traditionally relied on a market in health care are making greater use of regulation and planning. Equally, those countries which have traditionally relied on regulation and planning are moving towards a more competitive approach. In no country is there complete satisfaction with existing methods of financing and delivery, and everywhere there is a search for new policy instruments.

The aim of this series is to contribute to debate about the future of health services through an analysis of major issues in health policy. These issues have been chosen because they are both of current interest and of enduring importance. The series is intended to be accessible to students and informed lay readers as well as to specialists working in this field. The aim is to go beyond a textbook approach to health policy analysis and to encourage authors to move debate about their issue forward. In this sense, each book presents a summary of current research and thinking, and an exploration of future policy directions.

Professor Chris Ham
Director of Health Services Management Centre,
University of Birmingham

FOREWORD

Sir Raymond Hoffenberg

At the beginning of this analysis of the management of medical incompetence in Britain, Marilynn Rosenthal quotes from the preface to Shaw's *The Doctor's Dilemma* in which he chastises the profession for 'conspiring' to hide its own shortcomings. In his day medicine was certainly more of a closed shop than it is now. While there is still some reluctance to 'put the finger' on a colleague, inter-professional etiquette of this sort is overshadowed now by awareness of the need to ensure high standards of patient care. Elsewhere in the preface, Shaw says, 'As to the honour and conscience of doctors, they have as much as any other class of men, no more and no less'; he might easily have included 'competence'. In 1987, I wrote: 'There are doctors who are rude, inconsiderate, unsympathetic, even negligent . . . who are ill-informed or ignorant of modern medicine, whose judgement is inadequate, who make too many errors . . . who are simply incompetent'.[1] Doctors are no different from 'any other class of men' or women.

From my experience of medicine in Britain I suspect the number of doctors whose incompetence should cause concern is small but, as Marilynn Rosenthal points out, one cannot be certain. There is no systematic way of rooting out the poor performer, despite cogent reasons to do so. The first is a burgeoning awareness that medical standards vary and that the public is entitled to care within the NHS of a reasonably high standard; there is greater interest in litigation and compensation when things go wrong. Second, the competitive marketing philosophy of the 'new' NHS has introduced the need to improve outcome figures for medical intervention and, hence, to eliminate incompetence and inefficiency; the strengthening of managerial systems has given administrators the teeth to take action against a doctor whose performance appears not to match that of his

xii   *The incompetent doctor*

colleagues. How this is done is discussed at length in this book. The most important reason for wishing to improve standards of care lies within the concept of professionalism. As Dorothy Emmett has said, a profession 'carries with it the notion of a standard of performance . . . it has . . . a fiduciary trust to maintain certain standards . . . (partly) of competence or ability'.[2] As doctors we should have a professional interest in setting and maintaining high standards of practice.

To be fair, largely through the activities of the royal medical colleges in Britain, attempts have been made to improve these standards over a very long period. More than 40 years ago the Royal College of Obstetricians and Gynaecologists examined maternal obstetric deaths; for many years the Royal College of Physicians in London has carried out a series of outcome studies. In recent years the Confidential Enquiry into Postoperative Deaths (CEPOD) has attracted the participation of almost all UK surgeons, has pinpointed many of the reasons for poor outcome and has made recommendations for improvement.

While such general activities significantly enhance professional standards of excellence, procedures for dealing with individual 'problem doctors' are still tentative and idiosyncratic. Within most hospitals in the UK audit meetings take place that provide better information about the performance of individual doctors and departments. The Royal College of General Practitioners is trying through its own monitoring system to improve performance in its discipline. The weak link lies in private medical practice which is not subject to the same sort of scrutiny.

As Professor Rosenthal points out, much takes place behind closed doors: private discussions, friendly advice, collegial support, diversion of patients away from a potentially dangerous doctor or diversion of the doctor into a post with less direct responsibility for patient care; then, still within the private arena, a three or four wise men investigation or intervention by the appropriate royal college. Increasingly, managers wish to know more about the competence and efficiency of the doctors they employ, and remedial disciplinary action is now more frequently applied.

Professor Rosenthal has done her job extremely well. In an area in which there are few facts and figures, and those that exist are largely held in secret, she has had to rely on interviews, of which she conducted 60 in the UK alone. As one who went through the process, I know how tactfully, cleverly and searchingly she extracts her information. At a time of flux in the NHS, of flexing of managerial muscle, of distrust and suspicion between doctors and their employers, it took someone of Marilynn's ability and personality to produce such a clear picture of what is actually going on, and we should be grateful to her. I hope she will return at some time to review the position. I suspect much will have changed.

ACKNOWLEDGEMENTS

Certain opportunities, certain welcoming and generous people, certain organizations and institutions made this research and book possible. Without them, the task would have been infinitely more difficult, meagre, tedious and lonely. While I take full responsibility for interpretations and misinterpretations, for facts and for fictions, for inclusions and exclusions there are many thanks I owe, endless hospitality I look forward to reciprocating, and friendly support from which I have benefited.

A series of grants and awards were invaluable. These include a USA Fulbright Western European Region Research Grant (1989–90); University of Michigan Rackham Graduate School Faculty Enhancement Grant (1989–90); University of Michigan in Dearborn Vice-Chancellor's Grant (autumn, 1990); University of Michigan Office of the Vice-President for Research Small Projects Grant (autumn,1991); a British Council Travel Grant (1992); and a King Edward's Hospital Fund support grant (1992–93). To all these agencies and offices, my deep appreciation for your confidence in my original idea and its possibilities.

Support was also generously provided by the Centre for Sociolegal Studies, Wolfson College, Oxford, which provided not only office space and those precious resources no scholar can be without (Xerox, telephone, computer, fax), but also an intellectually stimulating atmosphere of international scope.

In Sweden, such services were graciously provided by the Swedish Planning and Rationalization Institute (SPRI) and the Swedish Medical Association. I had offices in both places and therefore benefited by the ease of contacts and the grace of two splendidly different environments and architectural surroundings.

Libraries and computer centres in cities across several continents were home to countless hours and days of writing. The University of Michigan Medical Library; the SPRI library in Stockholm; in Oxford the Bodleian Library, the Radcliffe Library, the Wolfson College Library; in New York City the Fordson Computer Center; in Hanover, New Hampshire, the general libraries, the Dana Medical Library and computer centres, and the Dartmouth Hitchcock Medical Center Health Science Library at Dartmouth College. I count myself especially fortunate to have enjoyed some of the best places in the world to think and write. May I thank those many librarians and computer consultants who were welcoming, helpful and interested.

Deserving thanks by itself is Wolfson College, Oxford. You who make Wolfson happen may be amused to know I have described it to friends and colleagues as 'Scholar's Paradise'. But please understand that early on, I contracted a serious and chronic case of 'Oxford fever', infected by the special grace and hospitality a Visiting Scholar finds at Wolfson. Everyone touched by that grace and hospitality, which pervades all the staff, knows its origin: Sir Raymond Hoffenberg who recently retired as president of the College. 'Bill' Hoffenberg personifies the warmth, charm, intelligence and good humour that only a few people in this life manage to bring together in one place and time. His early interest in my research, his ideas and reactions, his precious time, his patience with my long conversations, letters and queries were most supportive. I am honoured that he agreed to write the Foreword to this book. Thank you Bill, for all that and for the atmosphere you generated throughout Wolfson.

My thanks also go to Norma, Len and Margaret in the Wolfson porter's lodge; Carol Wratten in the Domestic Bursar's office; Mrs Walker, the college secretary; Adrian Hale, the librarian; Walter Sawyer, then head gardener; the cheerful maintenance men and laundry ladies . . . all of you help make Wolfson a special sanctuary for scholarship. Never change. From Common Room to laundry room, from Guest Nights to using the computer room at night, from the Dining Hall to the punt shed, from the croquet garden to the water garden, from the cheerful noise of the nursery school to the concerts in Haldane Hall, from the Tree Quad to the Harbour Quad, the Buttery to the Bar, I am grateful to have been a member, if only temporarily, of that community called Wolfson College.

Professor Deborah King, chair of the Sociology Department at Dartmouth College, made me welcome as a Visiting Scholar there as I finished the book. It couldn't have been a more felicitous environment. I found it ironic and edifying to have had a medical problem during my time at Dartmouth which kept me in the Dartmouth-Hitchcock Medical Center for five days. The hospital graciously provided me with a computer so that I could continue working on this book. During this period of time I was working on Chapter 6 'Empirical Research on Medical Mishaps and Mistakes'. Needless to say, my usual stream of questions to the good doctors who treated me tripled in volume, as did my anxiety levels. My thanks to all those doctors and nurses for their excellent care and patience. And to the staff at Dartmouth's Hanover Inn for all their kindnesses.

Many colleagues made arrangements for me or gave generously of their time to try and help me think through endless themes and details in this research. I list them alphabetically: David Armstrong, Johan Calltorp, Brendon Devlin, Robert Dingwall, Ray Fitzpatrick, Don Harris, John Horder, David Hughes, John Kotre, Michael O'Brian, Peter Pritchard, Rosemary Rue, Paul Sonda, David Taylor. I am a bit embarrassed to say how much I called on Ray Fitzpatrick.

And these are only the ones I am able to thank by name.

There are some 100 other individuals, in England and in Sweden, who lent me their time and their experience, their ideas and their insights about the difficulties of dealing with problem doctors. To all of them I have promised anonymity; without them this study would never have come to fruition. They trusted me, they confided in me; their experiences provide the stuff of this book. They know who they are. I deeply appreciate the gifts with which they entrusted me. I hope our work together will make it a little easier to help doctors with problems, and to provide patients the superior quality of patient care for which we all struggle.

A number of places were kind enough to invite me to give presentations at various stages of the study. I thank them all for the opportunity to test and explore ideas: the Centre for Sociolegal Studies at Wolfson College, Oxford, Don Harris, Director; The Institute for Health Policy at Southampton University, Professor Joan Higgins, Director; The Department of Health Administration at Erasmus University in Holland, Dr Aad Roo; the Sociology Department at Reading University; the Institute for Hospital Studies in Trondheim, Norway; SPRI in Stockholm, Sweden, Ingmar Ekerlund and Stephan Hakkanson; the Department of Social Medicine at Uppsala University, Sweden, Dr Eric Paulson; the Women's Research Club and the Women of the Faculty at the University of Michigan in Ann Arbor; the Behavioral Sciences Department at the University of Michigan in Dearborn.

Two research assistants made my work infinitely easier and more interesting: Margareta Bowallius in Stockholm and Angela Johnson in Oxford. Thank you for your enthusiastic and friendly help. Margareta has continued to send me material two years after the research was completed.

Helen and Carmen, Lenore and Marvin made life comfortable and provided magnificent New York cityscapes as I finished this book. Madeleine Jaye brought a brand new joy and deep delight with her arrival on 21 June 1993 at 1.07 a.m.

Ann Arbor, Michigan
Oxford, England
Hanover, New Hampshire

1

THE ISSUES: WHY
THEY ARE IMPORTANT

Two renowned social critics have provided powerful insights into the nature of self-regulation and the medical profession. The first, using the language of the social critic, said the following in 1902:

> Anyone who has ever known doctors well enough to hear medical shop talk, without reserve, knows that they are full of stories about each other's blunders and errors. . . . But no doctor dare accuse another of malpractice. He is not sure enough of his own [reputation] to ruin another man by it. . . . I do not blame him; I should do the same myself. But the effect of this state of things is to make the medical profession a conspiracy to hide its own shortcomings. No doubt the same may be said of all professions. They are all conspiracies against the laity and I do not suggest that the medical conspiracy is either better or worse than [others] but it may be less suspect.[1]

Some sixty years after Shaw wrote *The Doctor's Dilemma* and its analytic preface, the distinguished American sociologist Eliot Freidson, using the language of the social scientist, explained the nature of a high-status profession like medicine and the self-regulation that flows from it:

> As I noted in my analysis of medicine as a profession, autonomy is the test of that status. Professional people have the special privilege of freedom from the control of outsiders. Their privilege is justified by three claims. First, the claim is that there is such an unusual degree of skill and knowledge involved in professional work that nonprofessionals are not equipped to evaluate or regulate it. Second, it is claimed that professionals are responsible – that they may be trusted to

work conscientiously without supervision. Third, the claim is that the profession itself may be trusted to undertake the proper regulatory action on those rare occasions when an individual does not perform his work competently or ethically. The profession is the sole source of competence to recognize deviant performance and to regulate itself in general. *Its autonomy is justified and tested by its self-regulation.*[2]

Shaw's intuitive sense of how the profession copes with its 'blunders and errors' was an early effort to describe the way in which professional autonomy and self-regulation, systematically analysed by Freidson, actually function. Shaw did not 'trust [the profession] to undertake the proper regulatory action' in the face of an incompetent colleague. For Freidson, doing so is the ultimate justification of the large degree of autonomy granted to the profession of medicine by society. How accurate was Shaw in his assessment? How rigorously does the profession regulate itself? How justified is society in granting the medical profession significant degrees of autonomy?

The research described in this chapter adds to the discussion of these questions. It is a systematic, qualitative study of the informal coping mechanisms used by groups of doctors when a colleague shows signs of problematic behaviour. Consultant surgeons and senior general practitioners (GPs) in the British National Health Service (NHS) are the major focus of the study. However, other specialties are included, as are the roles of professional organizations, administrative units and managers who work with these doctors.[3]

WHAT IS A PROFESSION? WHY IS IT ALLOWED TO REGULATE ITSELF?

Among many who study the professions, including medicine, there is general agreement that occupations attaining the status of 'profession' have the following characteristics: they possess a systematic body of highly developed technical knowledge that is widely valued; strong standards of autonomy that emphasize self-regulation and altruism that submerge self-interest and emphasize service; the need for extensive authority over clients; a distinct occupational culture and collegial etiquette; and recognition of this professional status by political, social and economic leadership.[4] A few have suggested that a 'profession' is not a collection of such attributes, not an occupational group with high autonomy, but a strategy for developing and controlling a market for special services. An ethical ideal of service, monopoly over important knowledge and skills, and high social regard coalesce to establish high degrees of autonomy over work. The medical profession is an excellent example of a profession that brought these traits together to attain a market monopoly.[5]

Starr provides a social history of the profession of medicine in the United States and how it transformed itself with the developments in science, and the urbanization of the country, into a powerful group now increasingly challenged to prove its efficacy and its service orientation.[6]

The most sustained and comprehensive study of the medical profession is found in the work of the American sociologist, Eliot Freidson.[7] The focal point of his work is the intricate dynamics of professional power and autonomy. As noted in the quote from Freidson's work above, autonomy is the central characteristic of the profession. It is granted by the ultimate source of power in western societies: the state. The state grants the profession the legal right to regulate itself. It carries out this important task in a variety of ways.

Self-regulation

The process of 'self-regulation' has both formal and informal manifestations. The formal mechanisms are easily identified. They include selection for admission to medical school, systems of medical education and testing, registration (licensure), specialty credentialing and formal disciplinary activities. These are relatively visible organizations and processes in many societies.[8] In Britain, these responsibilities are shared by the General Medical Council (GMC) and the royal colleges. There are also governmental bodies that administer formal contractual arrangements, such as the Family Health Services Authority (FHSA) and the health authorities. And there are the various levels of managerial responsibilities of the NHS.

The criteria for entrance to medical school are potentially the most powerful tools for effective self-regulation the profession has. The characteristics of those admitted to medical education are a key basis for future behaviour. However, the tools of prediction, while improving, are not perfect, nor are they used rigorously or consistently. Social and ethical considerations are important; demographic considerations may shape the application pools. Furthermore, there are doctors practising in one country's health care system who have been chosen, socialized and educated in another culture.

Standards of education, testing and requirements for licensure are the most pervasive and obvious means for maintaining standards. The profession has expended enormous effort in establishing and maintaining educational programmes on the undergraduate, postgraduate and continuing education levels. The GMC and the royal colleges divide responsibility for various levels of medical education.

Registration permitting the practice of medicine is usually regulated by a governmental agency; in Britain it is the responsibility of the GMC.

There are regulations governing disciplinary procedures and there are stated codes of professional behaviour and etiquette. The GMC, empowered by Parliament to carry out these functions but financed and controlled by the profession, is a prime example of exclusively professional self-discipline and regulation.

These are the recognized mechanisms of professional self-regulation and, like all such social efforts, may perform reasonably well but work imperfectly, and require continuing attention and refinement. They change as external circumstances require.

Professional etiquette

Learning and maintaining appropriate collegial and professional behaviour is an intrinsic element of professional self-regulation and self-discipline. The inculcation of appropriate norms of behaviour, towards a colleague and as a professional, is as important as the science and art of medicine, although it is learned through a socialization process rather than classroom lectures. Through the behaviour of faculty, doctors on the wards, the informal exchange of experiences and observations, and the formal statements of professional organizations, students and young doctors learn what is expected of them as professionals and colleagues. Experienced doctors are presumably reminded of these norms throughout their careers.

In Britain, the most important formal statements governing professional and collegial behaviour are published in official documents of the GMC, particularly the 'Blue Book', *Professional Conduct and Discipline: Fitness to Practise*.[9] Here, doctors receive advice on standards of professional conduct and on medical ethics, the kinds of misconduct that may invoke discipline, the general disciplinary processes and those for impaired doctors. These are the formal codes of self-regulation. The manner in which they work and what they do and do not accomplish has been explored in previous studies.[10]

These codes change to reflect changing circumstances in the larger society.[11] As with most rules, regulations and laws, change is slow and must often catch up with already entrenched social practice. The most recent important example of an evolving code of behaviour is the delicate subject of criticizing colleagues. Traditional professional etiquette forbids such criticism. This deeply-held proscription has shaped collegial behaviour for more than 100 years. But current conditions have led the GMC to modify its stance on collegial criticism in important ways.

Until 1985, the official position on collegial criticism was straight-forward. 'The [GMC] also regards as capable of amounting to serious professional misconduct . . . [the] deprecation by a doctor of the professional skill, knowledge, qualifications or services of another doctor or doctors.[12]

No elaboration was deemed necessary for decades. Between 1987 and 1992, the Blue Book guidelines for norms of professional behaviour concerning disparagement and comment about one's professional colleagues underwent major revision. In 1989, the revised booklet stated:

> Disparagement of professional colleagues. It is improper for a doctor to disparage, whether directly or by implication, the professional skill, knowledge, qualifications or services of any other doctor, irrespective of whether this may result in his own professional advantage, and such disparagement may raise a question of serious professional misconduct. It is however entirely proper for a doctor, having carefully considered the advice and treatment offered to a patient by a colleague, in good faith to express a different opinion and to advise and assist the patient to seek an alternative source of medical care. The doctor must, however, always be able to justify such action as being in the patient's best medical interests. Furthermore, a doctor has a duty, where the circumstances so warrant, to inform an appropriate body about a professional colleague whose behaviour may have raised a question of serious professional misconduct, or whose fitness to practise may be seriously impaired by reason of a physical or mental condition. Similarly, a doctor may also comment on the professional performance of a colleague in respect of whom he acts as a referee.[13]

By 1992, the wording and approach to this issue is modified again, in response to the many changes in the NHS. Under 'Comments about professional colleagues', the Blue Book now states:

62. Doctors are frequently called upon to express a view about a colleague's professional practice. This may, for example, happen in the course of a medical audit or peer review procedure, or when a doctor is asked to give a reference about a colleague. It may also occur in a less direct and explicit way when a patient seeks a second opinion, specialist advice or an alternative form of treatment. Honest comment is entirely acceptable in such circumstances, provided that it is carefully considered and can be justified, that it is offered in good faith, and that it is intended to promote the best interests of patients.

63. Further, it is any doctor's duty, where the circumstances so warrant, to inform an appropriate person or Body about a colleague whose professional performance appears to be in some way deficient. Arrangements exist to deal with such problems, and they must be used in order to ensure that high standards of medical practice are maintained.

64. However, gratuitous and unsustainable comment which, whether directly or by implication, sets out to undermine trust in a professional colleague's knowledge or skill, is unethical.[14]

This important shift comes with the advent of medical audit at various levels of the NHS and as the GMC is asking Parliament to amend the Medical Act of 1983 to add a new disciplinary power for clinical incompetence. The latter will be discussed further in Chapter 7.

Other administrative regulations exist for disciplining hospital doctors and GPs. These include suspension from a specific hospital appointment and fines for breaches of general practitioner contracts. But the GMC alone holds the Register licensing doctors to practise and is the only body that can withdraw the licence to practise.

There are other forms of self-regulation as well, forms that are little seen and little known: informal approaches, informal mechanisms that take place behind the doors that close when doctors attempt to cope with problem colleagues.

INFORMAL SELF-REGULATION IN THE CLINICAL SETTING

There is little research on the informal mechanisms of professional self-regulation: those actions and procedures which are not required or written out in formal terms but are worked out in a set of informal processes to expedite and control daily work. Like all groups in a work setting, doctors do what any group of colleagues might do in the course of proceeding with their work. This includes dealing with the exigencies of someone who is faltering, unable or potentially unable to carry out work in a reasonable manner.

There may also be processes or mechanisms that are more formulated by suggestion rather than requirement. These shall be referred to as quasi-formal mechanisms. There is reason to believe that these informal and quasi-formal mechanisms are shaped by the same standards of professional etiquette and ethics that shape the formal mechanisms of professional and collegial self-regulation.

Systematic studies of informal approaches to medical professional self-regulation are rare. Two studies in the USA provide some insight: Freidson's *Doctoring Together* (1970) and Charles Bosk's *Forgive and Remember* (1979).[15]

A unique, landmark study which recognized the importance of informal processes is Charles Bosk's work on young surgical residents. He found an informal system that stressed adherence to basic norms of ethical and responsible behaviour.[16] A variety of techniques that emphasized hard work, responsibility for and rapport with patients, rapid reports of mistakes, learning from mistakes, sorted out those who continued with surgery and those who did not. Bosk observed, however, that once a doctor was 'certified' by this rigorous process (that is, had completed specialty training) there was no longer any 'corporate' (larger professional group) responsibility for coping with the incompetent surgeon.[17] Eliot Freidson has spent a career studying the professions, with a particular emphasis on the medical profession. One piece of research focused on an American group practice (an early staff model health maintenance organization where all the doctors were salaried staff) and found very little in the way of informal self-regulation.[18] Among colleagues, there was the withdrawal of favours. Any assertive action was carried out by someone in an official position. Essentially, problems were turned over to a reluctant administration.

The research described in the following pages builds on and expands the work of Freidson and Bosk, adding a cross-cultural dimension.

MEDICAL MISTAKES, 'PROBLEM' DOCTORS AND INCOMPETENCE

Defining a medical mistake or error is an enormous challenge. In the British Commonwealth[19] discussions of this subject usually employ the terminology 'medical misadventure', which encompasses 'medical error' and 'medical mishap'. A current, working, practical definition of medical errors is: errors of implementation and errors of ignorance.[20] Errors of implementation are problems that occur when utilizing what is known. Errors of ignorance means not having the necessary knowledge to carry out particular clinical procedures. These are professional attempts at definition; patients' views, of course, may be quite different.

However, any attempt at a definition is constrained by the shifting degrees of uncertainty in various specialties,[21] what may be a reasonable option given individual patient conditions, and factors in a particular kind of organizational setting. Bosk also points out that the definition may change depending on the stage in a doctor's career: student, resident, beginning an independent career, and experienced practitioner.[22]

It is one of the purposes of this study to see how 'mistake', 'error', 'mishap' are defined by practitioners themselves, this time with reference to experienced doctors: consultant surgeons and senior GPs. During the course of the interviews, no definition was offered, so that the thinking of the respondents would be revealed. In this manner, an image of the ways in which these particular members of the profession think about mistakes can be constructed.

In this study, 'problem' doctors include: impaired doctors by virtue of substance abuse, physical illness, mental illness, or manifestations of ageing; doctors whose knowledge or skills are poor by the standards of their peers; doctors who are 'burnt out', overworked or are having personal problems; doctors whose personalities and personal behaviour are seen as problematic in the work environment; doctors who may be having a 'run' of bad results. These categories emerge from the anecdotal cases collected in the course of the interviews carried out. It was generally thought, by the interviewees, that these categories of doctor are vulnerable to, or have the potential for, making mistakes.

Proposed here is a general definition of 'incompetence' which includes consistent, demonstrated lack of knowledge and/or skill in the conduct of clinical practice, and the production of below-standard outcomes. In reality, not all five categories of 'problem' doctor are clearly, consistently or necessarily incompetent.

There are many ambiguities and problems in all these definitions. What is of particular interest is how these terms are defined by members of the profession themselves as they carry out their work. Versions of this will be revealed through the anecdotes and interviews in the chapters to come.

METHODOLOGY: RESEARCHING THE 'DRAMA'

The study reported in this chapter was conducted in Britain (and Sweden) in 1990. It is qualitative, exploratory and ethnographic, based on in-depth, semi-structured interviews. It focuses on two categories of fully trained and experienced doctor: hospital consultant surgeons and senior general practitioners. Interviews were conducted with professors of surgery and general practice, consultant surgeons and senior GPs, nurses, managers of various rank, representatives of professional organizations and governmental units, and other appropriate experts. The author also consulted periodically with outside advisers to the project (see appendix).

The strength of this kind of research is the richness of detail gathered from such interviews. The weakness is the reliance on what interviewees say happened rather than on direct observation. Like most qualitative research, it is also difficult to replicate.

Like scientific research in general and ethnography in particular, maintaining objectivity is a goal and a challenge. I make no claims for greater or less objectivity than other social scientists describing a sub-culture. Having studied some of the formal mechanisms of self-regulation[23] and finding them important symbols but relatively minor as effective tools, it was reasonable to think about informal mechanisms, particularly since they have not been much studied, and in Britain and Sweden not at all. As the interest in quality assurance in medical care has grown[24] and more rigorous techniques for studying quality assurance are evolving, my hope is that holding a mirror to this corner of medical self-regulation might cast some light and open new corridors of research.

Some 60 in-depth interviews were conducted in Britain and 40 in Sweden. In Britain, interviewees were selected on the basis of the roles they occupied in two regions of the NHS. Each region has some of the best hospitals in the country; one region was more urban than the other and serves more minority populations. Those to be interviewed were solicited by letter with a description of the study, its objectives, and the topics to be covered. This was followed by a phone call requesting an appointment. Everyone contacted agreed to be interviewed. Several found the interview uncomfortable; the overwhelming majority were surprisingly frank and forthcoming despite the obvious delicacy of the subject.

The interview instrument included the following general categories of questions:

1 specific cases of 'problem' doctors and/or incompetence;
2 sources of information;
3 the informal mechanisms attempted and what blocked effectiveness;
4 the boundaries between avoidable and unavoidable mistakes and complications;
5 how impending NHS changes might affect these informal mechanisms.

As discussed above, no definition of mistakes, 'problem' doctors or 'incompetence' was offered to those interviewed, since it is the perception and definition of those involved themselves that must be understood in order to analyse when and how it is decided to take action with a faltering colleague.

The interview protocols were semi-structured in two ways. Topics rather than a series of specifically worded questions were raised consistently with each interviewee. The interviewer was always willing to follow whatever direction those interviewed wanted to take the topic for a reasonable length of time.

ABOUT THE ANECDOTAL CASES COLLECTED

The original intention of the study design was to collect anecdotal cases exclusively about consultant surgeons and senior GPs. While the majority are about these practitioners, many informants could not resist providing anecdotes about other specialties, from their own experience, and from other periods of time. This has been taken into consideration in Chapter 5, which summarizes the findings. Extensive notes were taken during each interview; these were summarized and analysed thereafter. Direct quotes are rendered as exactly as possible under these circumstances.

Cases were selected to illustrate particular points in the chapters that follow, but it will be clear to the reader that many cases illuminate a variety of analytical points, patterns of behaviour and determinants of those patterns.

It is also important to note that the anecdotal cases provide clues to the mechanisms used and other aspects of the analysis of these informal and quasi-formal processes. They are in no way a representative, random sample from a defined population of problem doctors. These are the cases collected within the limits of this particular study.

THE IMPORTANCE AND GUARANTEE OF ANONYMITY

No names of individuals were given in any anecdotal case reported. Every interviewee was scrupulously careful not to do so. No single person showed any inclination whatsoever to reveal names or any identifying characteristics. The names and positions of those interviewed were recorded in the original notes but no names are mentioned in order to protect identities. Only actual job titles remain so that the reader can locate perspective. Obviously, the nature of the subject demanded this approach; material could not have been collected without the guarantee of anonymity.

THE ADVANTAGE OF THE FOREIGN OBSERVER

Why would anyone be willing to talk to a researcher about such delicate subjects? A combination of factors explains the remarkable co-operation and openness encountered. The author is a foreign researcher, and certain advantages accrue from this. She will go away, for one, and is not identified with any institution or organization other than temporary academic affiliations. This is a burdensome subject, seldom discussed outside collegial circles. Perhaps it is a relief to discuss it with an interested and objective listener and outsider whose previous work on a related subject has been kindly received. Many of those interviewed expressed the hope that the study might contribute to improving how problem doctors are handled. It is widely recognized as a difficult and confounding challenge requiring greater understanding and more effective approaches. Finally, there was curiosity about what a systematic study might reveal.

BACKGROUND

The setting

It is useful to review, briefly, the organization of the British NHS at the time the original research was carried out. The NHS, created by an Act of Parliament in 1946, is a centrally organized, centrally financed health-care system to which access is a right of citizenship. Hospital doctors are salaried employees of the NHS, and salaries are the same across Britain for various levels of experience and responsibility (with geographical weighting). However, when a doctor reaches the top grade, consultant, he/she may be voted 'merit pay' by colleagues, which increases that individual's salary significantly. At this level, he/she may also engage in private practice.

General practitioners, on the other hand, are independent contractors who sign annual contracts for services to the NHS. The contracts are managed by Family Health Services Authorities (formerly Family Practitioner Committees). In the British NHS, the GPs are the gatekeepers to the hospital system. Patients go first to their GP, who decides if they require hospital care and then refers them to a particular hospital and consultant.

For administrative purposes, the NHS divides Britain into fourteen Regional Health Authorities (RHAs), each of which is divided into District Health Authorities (DHAs). The consultant contracts were administered at the RHA level, except in districts with medical schools and teaching hospitals where they were held at the DHA level. It is important to note one particular aspect of doctors' contracts in NHS hospitals: once a certain rank is reached, the contracts are for life.

Changes in the NHS

There have been a number of important organizational changes in the NHS in recent years. These are part of a long history of periodic reorganizations attempting to make it more effective and efficient.[25] The most recent changes were already in progress when the research was carried out in 1990. See Appendix 2.

The changes include the transformation of districts and providers into buyers and sellers of services to establish 'internal markets' in the hope of encouraging competition and efficiency; the establishment of free-standing 'trust' hospitals holding their own doctors' contracts, including those of consultants; self-selected general practitioner groups becoming 'budget-holders' and purchasing services for their lists of patients; Family Practitioner Committees transformed into Family Health Services Authorities (FHSA) with increased powers; medical audit a requirement in GP contracts; Medical Audit Committees required in each district; Crown Indemnity, making districts liable for medical malpractice. These and other impending changes taking place as this study is published, have created an atmosphere of transition in the NHS that some view as disconcerting confusion and others as stimulating opportunity.

Changes in the NHS and their potential impact on the issue of problem doctors, the use of informal mechanisms, thinking about mishaps and mistakes will be discussed in Chapter 7. What do the changes propose to accomplish? What has early empirical research reported? What is it likely they will actually accomplish?

The cast of characters

Certain individuals play important roles in the 'hidden drama' that is about to unfold, the use of informal mechanisms to cope with a fellow doctor who has become a problem or incompetent. For purposes of this study, we should note particular administrative positions: the Regional Director of Public Health (formerly the Regional Medical Officer), who held the consultant contracts (since the experience of the trusts who hold their consultants' contracts is so new and since the trusts appear to be continuing the traditional NHS consultant contracts for the time being, they are not included); the District Director of Public Health (formerly District Medical Officer), particularly in a teaching district; the Medical Staff Committee, an executive body representing the entire medical staff of a hospital. Its chair will play a role in handling problem doctors. Staff nurses and particularly head nurses; junior doctors in various training ranks; and on 'front stage' in the action will be doctor colleagues, fellow consultant surgeons and GPs who will slowly gather information, struggle with an assessment of the situation and 'develop a script' to cope with the problem doctor.

Also important are the Family Health Service Authorities administrators and lay chairs of their Medical Services Committees; the Local Medical Committee (LMC) executive secretaries and chairs; Community Health Council (CHC) executive secretaries; the now defunct Department of Health Regional Medical Officers; Department of Health (DoH) officials. Representatives of all of these have been interviewed.

The study produced material providing insight into how the medical profession views 'unanticipated complications', mishaps and mistakes, how information circulates and is assessed; the attempts to use the informal and quasi-formal mechanisms; where they are successful and where not; blocks to their effective use; relations between administrators and doctors and other related subjects.

This is an exploratory study on a little-researched subject. It is hoped this material will suggest further research, of both a qualitative and quantitative nature, in the same and related areas. This and future work can help the profession (and those working alongside the profession) gain greater insight into its own behaviour and suggest ways to improve the self-regulatory process in an environment (both national and international) where the profession is increasingly challenged to demonstrate that its autonomy is justified and that it carries on its self-regulatory function in an appropriate and useful way.

These are times of significant change in the NHS. Among the various goals of the Conservative government is more accountability from the medical profession. That pressure is complicated by a changing and more challenging public mood. Encouraged by external forces, the medical profession is looking for new ways to protect its autonomy, improve its standards, and better serve its patients. To examine what it does now, in the hidden acts of self-regulation, provides the basis for making those efforts more rigorous and effective.

The use of informal mechanisms is best understood by beginning with a discussion of how doctors, particularly consultant surgeons and general practitioners, think about their work and the prospects for mishaps and mistakes.

2

MAKING MISTAKES: HOW DOCTORS THINK ABOUT THIS

We're all entitled to mistakes aren't we? We're all vulnerable. 'There but for the grace of God go I. . . . I remember making that mistake myself.' Only doctors can judge doctors because we can immediately empathize. We are all human. There are problems in our lives that are not our fault. You come down to not punishing people except for intent. As long as you can say: 'That could happen to me', you are going to be sympathetic. You have to look at actual cases; we all have the right to err. But, the excessively repeated error is something else. A minority of doctors are repeating major errors and the formal system catches only some of them. A lot are never caught because it is hard to identify the errors and patients may not complain.
(General practitioner, 25 years' experience, active in national associations)

It is very difficult to define the boundary between the avoidable and unavoidable mistake. Surgeons are ordinary people really. It is a question of how far one can deviate from the average before it becomes so bad that action has to be taken . . . grossness, frequency . . . but it is very difficult to estimate. Vast numbers of things go wrong and are not reported. If something goes wrong, I want to know right away. [But] I get more and more forgiving as I get older.
(Consultant surgeon, 22 years' experience in teaching hospital)

THINKING ABOUT AVOIDABLE AND UNAVOIDABLE MISTAKES

The doctors in this study are treating patients on a daily basis. The GPs see dozens of patients in their offices and in patients' homes. Most patients have minor illnesses; some are seriously ill. The consultant surgeons are working with those, referred by the GPs, who require their special skills in the operating room.

Usually the care given is of good quality and, judged in the context of the millions of treatment and diagnostic transactions that take place in the NHS each year, most of the care is successful. None the less, adverse events, whether they be mistakes or accidents, happen.

As they diagnose and treat all these patients, how do doctors think about medical mistakes? The study explored this important question with all the medically trained interviewees by asking them to define the boundary between avoidable and unavoidable mistakes and to discuss their perceptions. General practitioners, consultant surgeons and medically trained administrators commented. A few non-medically trained hospital managers were asked as well as Community Health Council secretaries. All found the question both provocative and difficult.

The language of the question provoked considerable reaction when it was paraphrased using the terms 'acceptable–unacceptable' and 'reasonable–unreasonable' as well as 'mistakes' and 'accidents'. The universally preferred combination is 'avoidable and unavoidable accidents'. The language itself captures the essence of professional thinking about the subject.

While there are certain differences reflecting differences in work settings, in the experiences and perceptions of surgeons and GPs, there are enough commonalities to discuss a generic professional view. An analysis of all the responses reveals seven overarching, and recurrent themes: *permanent uncertainty; necessary fallibility; shared personal vulnerability; understanding and forgiveness; a norm of non-criticism; the egregious error;* and *the exclusivity of professional judgement.* The emergence of such common themes is striking.

Permanent uncertainty

A frequent first reaction is often a declaration that the boundaries are impossible to define, that so much of medical practice is uncertain and filled with risks. A consultant surgeon, who serves as one of the Three Wise Men for his hospital, says:

> Boundaries are very tough . . . the boundaries differ with specialty and with individual. What might be seen as unavoidable in the hands of one, might not be in the hands of another. Certain damage is accepted as unavoidable in some operations.

Of course, measuring the outcome of surgeons is easier than to show that physicians are negligent.

Many references to 'circumstances' are made, the common circumstances under which accidents can happen. Human limitations, patient and disease characteristics, organizational problems, fatigue and personal problems of the doctor, a good doctor caught in the middle of a bad treatment strategy: it is claimed all of these add to the intrinsic uncertainty of medical practice.

Setting the boundary between the avoidable and the unavoidable, according to a clinical director of surgery at a teaching hospital, 'is very difficult, it's impossible':

> How can anyone criticize a practice without knowing every case? The circumstances are always different. The patient and the clinical situation is always different. The boundary is always shifting.

As a Regional Director of Public Health put it:

> The circumstances of a mistake are critical. Errors arising from a situation where the personal conduct of a doctor was negative will attract more serious criticism. On the other hand, a very complex operation without appropriate support staff is different.

And, as expressed by a consultant anaesthesiologist:

> You can only define the boundaries [of avoidable and unavoidable accidents] in actual cases. In anaesthesiology, minor mistakes are happening all the time. There is a degree of subtlety that is pretty non-definable. Part of it is the ability to respond to chaos. Some chaps keep calm, have a depth of knowledge and a bit of a flair. But what's unacceptable? That's a problem. And 'every doggie is allowed a bite'. Hopefully you get enough insight to worry about yourself. There are some who you think are a disaster waiting to happen. Others, you have a good opinion of and . . . they make a mistake.

Or:

> There is this shifting border; there are circumstances where a mistake was avoidable but understandable at the same time. Nobody is better than 95 per cent of the time and you have to work hard for that. Typically, you get cumulative problems. Suddenly you find you are dealing with a completely unusual situation . . . you find yourself halfway through an operation

and realize you are doing it the wrong way. It was totally avoidable but you have committed yourself.

> (Consultant surgeon, teaching hospital)

This perception of uncertainty is shared by a number of experienced administrators as well. One FHSA manager expresses it this way:

> There was a GP who missed a meningitis diagnosis. This is very difficult to diagnose. And there is pressure on you as a GP not to over-admit to the hospital. This is a big issue: misdiagnosis.

Because of the widespread acceptance of uncertainty in medical practice, it is common to focus on how the doctor proceeded. A Local Medical Council secretary, himself a former GP with 25 years of clinical experience, expressed it well:

> The trouble with general practice is that 90 per cent of disease is self-limiting. You can tell patients anything. In the 10 per cent of things that require skill, the warning bells will ring. Any doubts and you will examine thoroughly even if you come up with a negative answer. The GP may make a wrong decision – OK, providing he has covered the ground. *Here* is the difficulty of incompetence and clinical judgement.

The focus on uncertainty and circumstances leads to two other frequent observations: the acceptability of variation of practice and the occasional conclusion that mistakes in practice do not exist. A district hospital consultant surgeon claims that:

> The borderline between [the avoidable and the unavoidable] is so vague. Disease processes and patients differ so enormously. Any two surgeons looking at the same problem may have different views.

A teaching hospital consultant surgeon not only agrees but stresses the importance of variation in practice:

> There are variations among us, variations in technique. This doesn't mean it is bad; just variations. Long may they last. A certain amount of heterogeneity is more creative.

A former Department of Health Regional Medical Officer and experienced clinician reveals how the theme of uncertainty in medicine is carried to its logical conclusion.

> GPs basically deny mistakes. They deny that there is any such thing. They won't recognize mistakes as part of daily practice.

If you talk about an unreasonable mistake, that can only be the result of a bad outcome.

When doctors think about mistakes or accidents in their practice, they emphasize the uncertainties, the importance of multiple mitigating circumstances, the existence of known risks; they accept the inevitable variability in practice. Their widespread preference for the term 'adverse events' for accidents can be understood.

It is ironic that, confronted with uncertainty as a central theme in medical work, doctors must also be authoritative. Inspiring confidence is essential in the encounter with patients. Patients want and need to believe in their doctors and what their doctors recommend. Belief in the doctor and trust in the doctor's advice can be an important part of the healing process. So the doctor must balance the appearance of certainty and authoritativeness with the over-arching knowledge of the uncertainties in the practice of medicine. Some doctors, of course, confuse authority with authoritarianism.

Necessary fallibility

If there is permanent uncertainty in everyday medical practice then there must be fallibility in what the doctor does. A well-trained doctor, respected by colleagues and engaged in acceptable, even superior practice, will expect to make mistakes in diagnosis, have accidents in the process of treatment and produce less than desirable outcomes for patients. Necessary fallibility[1] must be accepted as an intrinsic part of the practice of medicine.

One of the Regional Directors of Public Health put it poignantly.

I can remember mistakes I made. I will carry them to my grave. I can understand why I made them; I can live with them although in two cases, they were fatal. The first was in the 1950s when I was a junior doctor. I misprescribed for a patient and he died. The other patient was a woman whom I had examined on half a dozen occasions. I didn't detect anything unusual. She died of a brain tumour. I can understand how I failed to detect that. These are scars I carry always; all doctors carry these scars.

Shared personal vulnerability

It would be amazing if any doctor could put his hand on his heart and say: 'I have never made a very serious mistake on at least one occasion'.

(Regional Director of Public Health)

Along with the pervasive emphasis on the uncertainties of medical practice, sometimes carried to a denial of mistakes, many express a deep sense of shared personal vulnerability. Common expressions used throughout the interviews are 'That happened to me'; 'That could happen to me'; 'There but for the grace of God go I'. Doctors have a strong sense of identification with each other, enhanced by the mutually shared uncertainties of practice. That personal, unforgettable experience of doing something or failing to do something to a patient, with dire consequences, with minor consequences. All the interviewees could draw on their own experiences. An LMC chair with 25 years' clinical experience said:

> Mistakes anyone can make; those are acceptable. We all misdiagnose a simple complaint sometime. We fail to refer at an early stage, anyone can make this mistake; I've been known to make it. . . . You have to look at the level of the mistake. There could be a simple clinical mistake. A patient asks for an antibiotic. You write something wrong or the chemist can't interpret your writing. If that happens often you'd worry but it's acceptable once in a while because you're in a hurry. It's a basic mistake we are all prone to.

The mistakes one makes as a young doctor remain particularly vivid for some, and a powerful source of sympathy for one's fellow practitioners.

> When I was a young GP, a patient was brought in with heart failure. I thought she had a right-side heart failure which is treated differently than a left-side. There was no supervisor there and I had to make the decision. I did the wrong treatment. I made a mistake. She died. Was that incompetence? Where do you draw the line? If it's a genuine, one-off mistake, you're not going to do it again. If you are incompetent, you probably will. I don't know the answer to this. Perhaps it's possible to find if there is a pattern of mistakes. Look at complaints to see if there is a pattern.
>
> (Local Medical Council secretary)

Such experiences, shared by most if not all doctors, create a powerful pool of mutual empathy and an unforgettable sense of shared personal vulnerability. This binds the profession together in a unique fashion that underscores the sense of uncertainty. They have all experienced it and suffered. As a professor of general medicine puts it:

We would all use this subjective test: it could happen to me. This is a sort of collusion of professionals to stick together.

Such shared experience leads to the next common theme, although not always.

Understanding and forgiveness

Given the sense of permanent uncertainty, given the overwhelming feeling of shared personal vulnerability, it is not surprising that the interviewees express a strong impulse to understand their colleagues' situation when an accident occurs and are quick to forgive. A retired GP points out:

After all, doctors are trained to appreciate human frailty . . .

and one of the experienced Regional Officers of Public Health observes:

Mistakes exist because of human fallibility and colleagues realize there will be individual mistakes.

Understanding and forgiveness are easily offered, particularly if there is the appropriate quality of remorse.

A Family Health Services Authority manager talks about a junior doctor she knows well, revealing that even as a non-clinician, she accepts the norms of uncertainty, of shared vulnerability and of forgiveness.

There was a junior doctor – it was his second day as a registrar. He fails to check a drug that the nurse hands him. It was the wrong strength – too much. The patient could have been badly damaged. He had nightmares; it was a new situation and he was a knowing, caring, competent doctor. Every doctor I spoke to said they had done it themselves. You cannot strike off every doctor.

She has another anecdote:

A consultant operated on the wrong eye. This was his first mistake ever. He comes to the administration office and reports his own mistake. He personally tells the patient. He

admits total liability. Luckily, it's not permanent damage; up to
a certain amount of damage is acceptable.

A Regional Director of Public Health, after describing an accident,
says:

> The individual doctor feels dreadful; thinks it over; may
> present the case and admit the mistake; and even discuss it with
> the patient's family. This is quite often done in intensive care.
> With so many procedures, there are limits to a doctor's skill.

Those interviewed put a strong emphasis, not only on the personal quality of remorse but also on appropriate behaviour and
procedures. A professor of general practice elaborates:

> In terms of an individual case, the boundary [between the
> acceptable and the unacceptable] is drawn by an assessment of
> whether the GP has behaved properly. Has there been a sense
> of responsibility? Does he have the insight to recognize his
> mistakes? Does he have insight when challenged?

Another academic GP (a regional adviser) observes:

> There is the question of honesty, openness and constructive
> criticism. We have to know what our weaknesses are and be
> willing to do something about them.

The egregious error

But even the norm of understanding and forgiveness has its limits.
There are enormously generous boundaries for forgiveness, yet
grossness and frequency of error, lack of insight and ability to learn
from a mistake, and quality of interpersonal relationships sometimes combine to limit understanding and forgiveness.

> Something quite severe can be acceptable but only if it happens
> once. If it happens twice . . . !
>
> (RDPH)
>
> It is a question of how far one can deviate from the average
> before it becomes so bad that action has to be taken . . .
> grossness, frequency . . . but it's very difficult to estimate.
>
> (Consultant surgeon)
>
> Unacceptable is when it happens consistently.
>
> (GP of 20 years' experience)
>
> This is a very difficult question. There could be a misdiagnosis;
> the wrong artery is cut. Somehow these are accepted as errors

of judgement as long as they are one-off. People know this happens. Yet if it is a regular occurrence, that is a different matter.

(District nursing officer)

Arrogance is the worst thing. A consultant surgeon removed the wrong hand of a woman diabetic in her late 60s, early 70s. It was a totally mismanaged case. The hand had gangrene. The consultant was shilly-shallying; he said it was a perfectly understandable mistake. The family wanted an apology and a stern letter of reprimand. The hospital acknowledged the mistake but offered no apology. It went to the Secretary of State who issued a stern reprimand and the family got damages from the District.

(CC secretary)

Repetition, degree, insight, commonality – these set the boundaries between the acceptable and the unacceptable mistake. Are they repeatedly made? Is the person able to learn from his mistakes?

(GP regional adviser)

It becomes unacceptable when they don't learn from their mistakes. It could happen to anyone once, maybe twice, but no more.

(RDPH)

It's easy for a group of colleagues to accept frequency because they think it is an accepted outcome for a certain procedure, perhaps an experimental procedure.

(Hospital manager)

It just has to be horrendous for anything to be done.

(FHSA manager)

Like a small amount of stealing is OK, a small mistake is OK. The really outrageous incident is unacceptable.

(CHC secretary)

Occasionally, the judgement isn't so lenient.

Sometimes just one case requires discipline. A patient was transferred to the —— from another hospital. The case started with termination of a pregnancy and ended with surgical mayhem. It was very bad. This requires discipline; it will get turned over to the courts. There will be a substantial settlement.

> (Consultant surgeon and national expert)

This is a rare reaction.

> It is very subjective, how you judge incompetence. How incompetent do you have to be before someone intervenes? It's very subjective, based on degree of wrongness and badness.
>
> (GP of 40 years' experience)

Unacceptable frequency, grossness of the mistake, or repeated failure to follow clinically appropriate procedures, a pattern of mistakes, can lead to criticism. But even these are bound by a number of constraints, particularly personal relationships. A CHC secretary observes:

> Some of the decisions must be personal. If you are an 'OK' colleague, you'll be covered when you're in trouble. Do you belong to the same golf club? Masonic lodge? Did you go to the same boarding school? Do you meet somewhere socially? Especially with older doctors but this might be changing now. Women and overseas doctors are more vulnerable to being criticized. Lots are locums. But after all, I don't complain about appalling CHC secretaries.

An FHSA manager states:

> It depends how your colleagues play it. If they are supportive, they will play it down.

One of the former Regional Directors of Public Health also pointed to a mix of objective and subjective standards.

> Doctors look at outcomes for a disease in a particular age group and say: 'The outcomes of Doctor B in fifty-year-old women are not as good as we would expect.' If people get a 10 per cent worse result, questions come up; if it widens to 15–20 per cent, something is really wrong. But you need a large population of patients to make these judgements. Groups of consultants do this on a regular basis, informally, as they chat among themselves. Juniors do this all the time. This gets passed around and reaches the consultants. But there are no specific rules. Personality is important. The acceptable and the unacceptable line

shifts depending on personality and relationships. When doctors eat lunch, they are exchanging ideas about what to do with various patients. They are developing a knowledge hierarchy.

A tiny number of those interviewed pointed to more specific criteria for distinguishing between the acceptable and the unacceptable. These include the law, community standards or empirical research. One GP, in practice 40 years and active in his LMC, says:

> The yardstick for determining the boundary between the acceptable and the unacceptable is the law. Is this something that an average, competent colleague would do? Not the best; what would the average doctor do? It has to be a rational and reasonable judgement. The standard shouldn't be a 'perfect' decision.

Another practising GP concurs:

> The boundary between acceptable and unacceptable is a question of skill and judgement in using skill. There has to be an adherence to what a responsible body would support. There is variability in medical practice but we can be judged on a basic standard, not the best standard.

One surgeon, involved as expert witness in court cases, is not so sure.

> Mistakes are *extremely* difficult to define. I do a great deal of medico-legal work and the criterion I use is: is this part of qualifying, core knowledge to become a specialist? But there are occasions when you have to allow for personality and the conduct of the patient.

Everyone seems to agree that the egregious error is difficult to accept but even here a number of factors may mitigate a harsh response.

The norm of non-criticism

According to a professor emeritus of surgery:

> In [Britain] we tend to turn our backs on these things. Therefore it is not easy to recall where people were willing to confront incompetence.

This observation reflects a common theme. Where uncertainty confronts all members of the profession daily and all see themselves vulnerable to accidents, it is not difficult to understand a tacit norm of non-criticism, a conspiracy of tolerance. This is recognized and accepted by administrators as well.

> There is terrific reluctance, on the part of all sorts, to condemn and criticize. Much of medical practice success depends on faith and, if it is undermined, the treatment could suffer. There is fear of affecting a doctor's livelihood; there is the natural reluctance to criticize.
>
> (FHSA complaints officer)

> Do GPs cover up for each other? I am sure that could be the case. Don't we cover up for our own family? It's a human thing. Without it, it would lead to poor functioning of a partnership. These are businesses and such things could affect the whole organization of practice. If they don't support each other, the whole balance of science could be affected.
>
> (Retired FHSA administrator)

> Groups of specialists develop a very strong group feeling together, particularly small groups . . . and this inhibits criticism.
>
> (RDPH, retired)

> Doctors overwhelmingly cover up for each other on these matters. There are very strong group feelings that depend on colleague relationships. If the relationships are good, they cover up, if they are bad, they won't and it comes to the RDPH. But the doctors won't let a really bad doctor continue; it brings a bad reputation to the hospital and to them.

A FHSA manager points out another source of non-criticism: loyal patients.

> It never ceases to amaze me how few complaints we get about the one we know to be incompetent. People are so resistant to complaining. Why don't people complain? Is the system too difficult? Is there no faith in the system? Are their expectations so low? What about basic principles of fairness?

Patients' loyalty and willingness to tolerate a great deal from a doctor with whom they have long and satisfying rapport is a variation of professional non-criticism that some patients have accepted. Patient ignorance may also be a factor.

The exclusivity of professional judgement

There is one additional theme that comes out of the interviews: that only the profession itself can make judgements about clinical accidents and mistakes.

It is the cumulative logic of permanent uncertainty, necessary fallibility, shared personal vulnerability, understanding and forgiveness, the eventual recognition of the egregious error and noncriticism that leads to the firm and common conclusion that only the profession can judge the clinical and professional behaviour of its members. At the same time, there is ready recognition of how difficult this is to do.

> Mistakes exist because of human fallibility and colleagues realize there will be individual mistakes . . . frequency, complexity, severity are most important but these would be peer judgements.
>
> (Regional Director of Public Health)

> There is the question of honesty, openness and constructive criticism. We have to know what our weaknesses are and be willing to do something about them. It's easiest to address these issues among peers. It's a question of doing or failing to do what is right. That which I should know; the standard knowledge for GPs. But there is knowledge uncertainty. What counts is why one does something and how one thinks.
>
> (Academic regional GP adviser)

> In the twelve years I've been here, I've heard something a half dozen times. I see the chair of the medical staff weekly but not on competence issues. Of course, all the districts differ but this one stands out because of the tight cohesiveness of the medical staff. They are a self-regulating, self-conducting medical group. They keep these issues and all issues to themselves.
>
> (Non-teaching district manager)

One unit manager at a well-known teaching hospital confides:

> It is difficult for me, not having a medical background at all. I have to rely wholly on the appropriate consultants. I simply don't have the knowledge and training.

And his colleague says:

> I don't know where the line [between the acceptable and the unacceptable mistake] lies. I am keen to examine closely the

tendencies to cover up medical negligence. That line moves up more than down.

An academic hospital general manager notes:

There is a newly appointed consultant, here just two years. In the last ten days I have been hearing about his ability to cope. He may not be appropriately treating patients. Is he too conservative? I don't know; they say he is incompetent. I have heard it from a clinical director who has asked what to do. There have been discussions with the chap. I suggested that the director talk to others on the firm and get back to me. I believe he is under stress and is anxious. He's unhappy in the job. If I were faced with a group of colleagues feeling that he has not acted properly, I'd get him in for a frank talk. If that didn't help and there was evidence of incompetence . . . there would be difficulty getting that . . . I would have to take advice about what line to take . . . It is not for a general manager to make judgements about clinical skills. I'd have to rely on other experts to tell me what he was doing was right . . . outside professional judgement. That could only happen if someone made a complaint. And I bet my bottom dollar that they wouldn't. Doctors are very reticent unless it is something that is really dangerous for the patient. I think there is a change of tide; young consultants are more likely to do so than the old guard. But there is still a medical Mafia, real protection. 'Let's stand shoulder to shoulder.'

Only peers can judge, but it is recognized that there are things that stand in the way of peer judgement – differences of expert opinion and the deep-seated reticence to criticize each other for all the reasons already discussed.

There is nothing formalized. At the end of the day, there are differences of opinion. In the courts you see equal experts disagree.

(Consultant surgeon)

Serious mistakes are when several things go wrong at the same time. The easiest to deal with is what everyone would regard as a mistake . . . 'bad practice' . . . we would try to stop this. But there again, these things are so much a matter of judgement and it is so very difficult to make a judgement. The grossest things are easiest to agree upon but lots of these things are never detected by patients.

(Consultant oncologist)

These two statements reflect the theme of uncertainty and the tendency of the profession to close ranks because each individual sees himself in the tragedy of each colleague's mistakes.

The hesitancy to criticize is reflected in other observations. A GP of 35 years' experience says:

> Mistakes anyone can make; those are acceptable. We all misdiagnose a simple complaint sometimes. We fail to refer at an early stage. Anyone can make this mistake; I've been known to make it. It becomes unacceptable when it's too gross – to miss breast cancer, for example. Doctors should be reprimanded but no one likes to do this . . . we're protective, perhaps too protective.

The District Medical Officer in a teaching district puts it in another way:

> Among consultants, they would take the peer group standard as a measure. Anything not up to this would be unacceptable. But in a sense, we don't pursue acceptable and unacceptable at all. I don't think the surgeons ever think in this way.

An experienced GP captures a common sentiment among doctors:

> If we criticize, we'll be criticized. It's all so marginal; it's difficult. GPs are not good at confronting a colleague, and those who are incompetent isolate themselves. If we all complained about each other all the time, we're all vulnerable.

A professor of surgery (retired) states:

> It seemed clear to me, as head of a department, you'd generate more friction by criticizing others. Better to lead by example. And this spills over into investigating complaints as a Wise Man. Once you became head of department, you were responsible only to yourself. Most tend to sweep things under the carpet.

There is firm agreement, shared even by managers, that only the profession can pass judgement but it is constrained not to do so for a variety of understandable but confounding reasons: it is contrary to norms of peer collegiality to criticize; it is difficult to carry out demanding work without an atmosphere of strong collegial support; there are so many uncertainties in most specialties that it is impossible to be certain that criticisms are justified when even equal experts disagree. After all, criticism could jeopardize a person's livelihood; it is human to protect each other.

All agree on the exclusivity of professional judgement. However, all the elements that shape the profession's thinking – uncertainty, shared vulnerability, understanding and forgiveness, non-criticism – encircle and constrain judgement of one's colleagues.

PREVIOUS RESEARCH

Other research, particularly from the United States, documents similar themes in how doctors think about their work, their mistakes and competence.

Renee Fox's pioneering study of medical students established the importance of learning to appreciate and live with uncertainty in medical work.[2] Her analysis points to three kinds of uncertainty: the indeterminacy and uncertainty of professional knowledge; incomplete mastery of available knowledge which the student finds overwhelming; and not being able to distinguish between imperfect mastery of knowledge and imperfections in the knowledge itself.

Rue Bucher and Joan Stelling's studies of medical students build on Fox's work and describe the need, therefore, to emphasize the process of work.

> Given the tenuous nature of much professional knowledge, it is perhaps not surprising that the trainees, in evaluating themselves and others, come to give greater emphasis to the actual process of doing their work than to the results of the process. If one is doing the right thing, one is practicing competently.[3]

Bosk's study of surgical residents[4] (and Light's work on psychiatric residents) documents the emphasis on learning the proper way of behaving in the face of continual clinical uncertainty. Technical errors are forgiven if the behaviour around them is appropriate: reporting problems immediately, interacting with patients and their families in proper ways, learning from the experience. As Light puts it:

> In the professional world, one can make a mistake in technique without it affecting outcome or one can have perfect technique with poor results. Only when poor results can be directly attributed to technique does outcome contribute to the definition of a mistake and often this is not the case. Residents in psychiatry and internal medicine could not define mistakes in their work because the layman's ideas of mistake had become foreign to them through professional training. When something happens that might look like a mistake, professionals

enact specific rituals (like mortality review) which have features designed to deflect or mollify charges of bad practice.[5]

In the latter, he is referring to the Bosk study.[6]

In a more recent article, Bosk tries to define medical error and
begins by noting four limitations to any definition: chronic uncertainty; variability in specialty between doctor's action and
patient's response; observability of doctor's practice; and the stage
of a doctor's career.[7] In medical school, students are rewarded for
intellectual correctness; during residency, two kinds of error based
on the clinical management of patients are recognized: innocent
errors that are quickly recognized, reported and learned from; and
blameworthy errors that are covered up.

As for the senior doctor, Bosk suggests that what was proper
surveillance of a resident is illegitimate meddling in the affairs of a
peer. Senior doctors are not criticized by their peers but judged in
terms of style, philosophy and personality. If a doctor has internal-
ized the norms of proper behaviour, actual mistakes are generally
ignored. He deplores the lack of corporate responsibility for errors
and competence.[8]

Bosk's work is based on studies in the United States. But his
findings and those of others are clearly echoed in the thinking of
British doctors interviewed in this study, beginning with the theme
of uncertainty. These ways of thinking and behaving are embedded
in modern medical training and what is considered the nature of
modern medical practice itself. They transcend geographic borders
and different health-care systems.

What about British doctors who have long worked in a highly
corporatized health-care system, the NHS? Does this make a
difference in how they respond to specific cases of problem colleagues? Their framework for thinking is the same; do the circumstances of their work environment promote different, more
collective responses? This will be addressed in Chapter 3.

WHEN IS A DOCTOR A PROBLEM? WHEN IS THE PROBLEM INCOMPETENCE?

A Local Medical Council secretary describes a recent case:

> I held the hand of a doctor a week ago; sensible, well-qualified,
> young. He was called to see a patient of one of his colleagues;
> he'd never seen him before. The complaint was pain in the
> shoulder (the widow says pain in the chest; the doctor denies

this). The GP examines him thoroughly and can't find anything. He concludes it was a musculature strain. The pain gets better and the man drops dead after three days. The family says the GP should have done more. There was a hearing at which the GP said: 'Yes, I should have done more, it's clear he did have a heart attack.' Is this doctor incompetent? My view is no, he made a mistake. If it's a genuine, one-off mistake, he's not going to do it again.

The unit manager of a large academic hospital says:

I heard from the nursing side that a cardiac bypass patient got the wrong blood group. I went right down to see the consultant. He was a very competent guy. This was a genuine mistake. This happened through the over-pressure of work. I assessed that the family wasn't going to sue unless they were 'guided'.

The chair of a local LMC describes a long-term case.

For ten years, in a small town, there were troubles with a doctor who took on a practice. He had a marvellous CV and glowing references . . . probably to get rid of him. He's been having difficulty taking on a partner. He's kicked out partners three times; each one lasts about a year. I've had occasion to talk to him like a grandfather. The partners come in without an agreement. We're worried and are keeping an eye on this.

A new hospital manager in a large urban teaching hospital reports a well-known case of two cardiothoracic surgeons at this hospital who have hated each other. Their work relationships have been appalling. They were out to destroy each other and it was destroying the unit. The Royal College took away accreditation for a senior registrar post. They were continually calling each other's clinical judgement into question. There were all sorts of investigations, Three Wise Men and external. It went on for ten years and there were many futile attempts to resolve it. It only stopped because one retired.

A recently retired RDPH says:

This case involved a diagnostic specialty. Incompetence was alleged by virtue of a personality defect. There was widespread criticism that this person's technical work couldn't be faulted but that he was incapable because of an awful personality. Such a dreadful personality that he couldn't do the job. An extreme case of rudeness and brusqueness. This resulted in long professional, legal and administrative battles. The process took two or three years and he was eventually completely exonerated.

An academic hospital manager recalls:

> There was this somewhat older cardiovascular surgeon. He was getting slower than he ought to be. The theatre staff became frustrated; they felt it wasn't good for the patients. This just went on for several years until he got to retirement age.

An experienced consultant surgeon in a district hospital says:

> In recent years, a number of consultants nearing retirement have had difficulties . . . possibly burnout. They are between 60 and 65 but they are not incompetent. . . . Surgery is demanding and there may be limits to a person's capacity. In a hospital like this we don't often watch each other operate. But one hears from the anaesthesiologist, the juniors and the senior nurses who might hint at a problem. . . . Not really pulling your weight implies possible incompetence. There comes a period of time when your knowledge diminishes. If you are in a rut, after twenty years in post, you get bored. Never keep up, never keep abreast; don't attend department and education meetings.

An LMC secretary tells about

> . . . the most unusual and longest case we had. It involved a GP who started practice here in 1978 and who finally retired in 1986. He was a totally incompetent, charming man who was muddled and inefficient. He started off with drugs and drink, and complaints started to come in 1979. By 1982, he ended up in front of the General Medical Council. He wasn't suspended then but referred to their Health Committee. And there was the promise that the LMC secretary (me) would watch over him. He reported back to the Health Committee every six months and promised not to take drugs and drink. The LMC considered it a great triumph to get this done. Because he was closely monitored by his colleagues, they let him scrape by. But by 1986, he was suspended by the GMC. He appealed because he 'wanted his name back' before he retired. And he had a money problem. He hadn't been working that long and hadn't much of a pension. He was a lovely chap, much manipulated by his patients. What terrible problems. Besides drugs and drink, he didn't return medical records, he wrote a prescription when

he was suspended. He was told by the FHSA, the LMC, by me that he *had* to retire and he did in late 1986.

The former chair of a large city LMC tells of a case that came out at an FPC meeting two years ago:

> A number of complaints had been received about a single-handed general practitioner with poor premises, a man in his late sixties. The FPC has an inspection procedure for premises. The FPC secretary arrived, with a colleague, at these shabby premises. There was chaos, and they were able to secure the doctor's resignation on the spot. The FPC could have threatened him with an MSC case or not to pay the premises allowance. I don't know if this doctor was incompetent. How do you judge incompetence? How 'incompetent' do you have to be before someone intervenes? When you treat wrongly? Badly? It's very subjective.

A District Director of Public Health spoke of

> a nationally known psychiatrist with an alcohol problem. He got no support from his peer group. He was allowed to go on until retirement . . . four years. He could have retired early but there was no major accident, no litigation, no complaints that came to my level.

A Regional Director of Public Health tells of another case that involved an anaesthesiologist who was beginning to show signs of incompetence through taking drugs. He had a long term chronic back injury. There is not yet specific evidence, just anxiety.

An LMC secretary confides:

> I wrote to the GMC once about a very good doctor who went on holiday. His two partners engaged an unknown locum who was called to visit an elderly lady. She had an accident and had a fractured neck. The locum went but didn't examine her; he was incompetent. The principal of the practice was found in breach and had a large penalty. The FHSA found that the locum had been a principal in another area and had retired because of ill health. The FHSA and I wrote to the GMC. It took them months and months, nine months to decide what to do with him. They said the poor doctor was under psychiatric care and recommended that he work in a partnership where he

can be supervised. It all happened a year ago. I think this is ridiculous. They should have suspended him.

He went on with another story.

This case involves a sweet guy taken into partnership by a very forceful GP. He was a 'yes' man. After two years, the senior partner died and he has now been running the practice for three years and is forever ringing us up with silly questions. He's incompetent, doesn't know medicine. He's not British. Not one colleague has a good thing to say about him. Not only is he incompetent but inefficient on the business part of the practice. This weak, incompetent doctor has never been complained against. The problem there is that the patients tend to be simple folks, an ethnic minority dictated to by the doctor who is an authority figure.

A Regional Director of Public Health says:

Here's a case I just heard of last week. There are concerns that a particular orthopaedic surgeon is undertaking cases and producing very bad results. He is relatively young and well trained. But he is having more than a little run of bad luck. He is in a specialized field and is doing work outside his range of competence. The outcomes have been less than satisfactory in a number of instances.

An academic health manager told the following story:

The very articulate father of a patient who died complained directly to the head manager who talked to me. I agreed we should call for the case notes. We found the complaint had several features that indicated true incompetence on the part of one consultant and poor management on the part of all the doctors. This was regarding a complex head injury. We asked another very senior consultant for a confidential report. He did that after speaking to the consultants and the junior doctors. He recommended certain actions but no formal procedures.

The former LMC chair tells about an experience he had.

My practice has two in the group. We employed a part-time assistant who was very energetic and full of ideas. After a while, he approached us with a money-making scheme for being a third partner. We moved slowly so he went elsewhere and we lost touch with him. We later found out that he was prescribing to drug addicts for money. He appeared in a police action when a patient was charged with assaulting him. He employed a bouncer in his waiting room to keep order. Next, he was due to be charged by the police and the GMC. He was found to be unable to plead because of mental problems – manic depression. I think he committed suicide. I think most doctors who are incompetent are tinged with mental illness. Anyone who qualifies in the UK has a pretty high IQ. The ones who break down are those under strain.

When is a doctor a problem? When is the problem incompetence? These colleagues and administrators are identifying a wide variety of problems when speaking about troublesome or faltering doctors. They present a continuum of problems: inexperience and work pressure; interpersonal or personality conflicts; growing old and impairment; apparent lack of knowledge or skill; criminal behaviour. All these doctors are identified as being problems. Which are incompetent? And by what criteria? Which doctors are making mistakes?

If we begin with mistakes, the most devastating are those of the most inexperienced doctors and of the best doctors: the missed fatal heart attack; the error over blood group. Bad results associated with suspect professional behaviour are a separate category. Every other doctor is suspect for mistakes. The ageing, the alcoholic, the medicated, the obnoxious personality, the hated colleague, the criminal. Most anecdotes involve suspected incompetence; most do not involve patient complaints. Those that are accused directly of incompetence often have overt characteristics that arouse suspicion: they are disorganized, abrupt, difficult. Problem colleagues and mistakes seem to emerge in the following ways: clear mishaps or mistakes by someone who is professionally competent; clear mishaps or mistakes by someone who is professionally suspect; suspect characteristics; unprofessional behaviour. Certainly suspect characteristics may merit attention but the ambiguities, confusions, and intertwining of a number of issues that may or may not relate to incompetence, in its full sense, begin to reveal themselves in these cases.

Are all impaired doctors incompetent and making mistakes? The ageing doctor? The alcoholic? The drug addict? The suspected mentally impaired? The physically impaired? The doctor on medication? What about the doctor who is breaking the law or the one whose personality conflicts with others in the workplace? While it is probable that some of these doctors are making mistakes some of the time, this is more a presumption than documented fact. Are

they making more mistakes or having more mishaps that we now
see are considered part of clinical practice? Some of these doctors
are offending professional sensibilities and professional norms;
some are growing tired or bored. Some are approaching the end
of their careers without great self-insight as to fading skills. There
is no clear-cut standard for competence; there is no clear-cut way
to distinguish between accidents, mishaps, mistakes, errors, at
least not in the thinking and experience of most of those
interviewed.

An LMC secretary tries to think through these dilemmas.

> Incompetence is not always synonymous with ill health. A GP
> can be not up to date, or can be lazy. It is very difficult to draw a
> hard-and-fast line. My remit is really to look after the sick ones
> and this is true of all the LMCs. Unless there are standards,
> guidelines about incompetence, there is nothing we can do.
> The profession now realizes that it has to do it itself or the
> government will do it. The GMC is aware of this problem. I and
> several of my colleagues had dinner with the president of the
> GMC. He asked us what should be done about the incom-
> petent doctor. We told him we see a lot of incompetence – GPs
> qualified thirty-five years ago. There is nothing that says they
> have to appear in front of their peers to say they are still
> competent.
>
> The MSC hearings are more and more raising questions of
> competence, not to establish a mistake but to see if terms of the
> contract are carried out. It is difficult to draw a line between a
> breach and incompetence. I see cases where I think they are
> incompetent. You try, in devious ways, to say [the GP] might
> look at his standards of practice. There is nothing I can do
> about incompetence; just wait for the next mistake. I can do
> something about sickness but I'm not an academic to say
> whether he's incompetent or not. There *should* be some
> monitoring standards.

A Department of Health complaints specialist expressed it this
way:

> There are less than 5 per cent of doctors who are clinically
> incompetent. But this is very difficult to determine. They are
> unable to take a history; they're unable to diagnose in
> certain situations. They can't cope with uncertainty. They
> are bad managers and communicators. They are likely to be

single-handed and out of the information networks. GPs natur-
ally group themselves by level of competence so that the less
competent are influencing each other.

An FHSA manager (in a large urban area) who says she is unable to
identify the boundary between acceptable and unacceptable mistakes, added another characteristic.

They are very elderly . . . perhaps impaired by alcohol, drugs,
mental or physical illness. They have little continuing medical
education.

She agrees that they are usually single-handed but adds that some of
the best GPs are also single-handed.

A former Department of Health Regional Medical Officer
(whose job it was to visit GP practices for official purposes) also sees
single-handed practices as a

danger area. They can get away with catastrophe. They can't
be detected; nobody knows. If they have been taking care of a
family for forty years, the family won't complain. In a group
practice, they are able to sift to each partner's strengths. If they
have a good, close, stable relationship, they help and advise
each other.

Among the tiny handful who see these issues in a different and
more rigorous way is a university GP reader who is helping develop
GP standards of practice.

It is difficult to define what is a mistake. But we are now looking
at quality assurance and audit. We are moving towards a
consensus of what we should be doing, that is, standards of
practice. This department has been promoting prevention in
general practice, for example, recording of blood pressure. In a
study, only a minority of patient records recorded blood pressure having been taken . . . then the patient has a stroke.

A consultant surgeon at an academic centre says:

Boundaries (between the acceptable and unacceptable) are
drawn by audit and statistical information. A 25 per cent
infection rate in hernia operations is not good. Well-
recognized patterns are becoming more recognized. If one unit
has more infections than another, we need to identify the facts
and analyse the cause of this. It may be the population you are
working with . . . there will always be variations . . . it's

fearfully difficult to identify small variations. They aren't that important. The big ones are important. Audit should be part of ordinary practice; that's why it is in the White Paper.

A clinical director of surgery thinks along these lines as well.

You need statistical or corroborative evidence. In my specialty, there never should be [organ] damage. I do a hundred operations a year and get a 1 per cent damage rate – one or two a year. There are always a percentage who suffer this injury.

Another consultant surgeon notes:

Will these problems arise more often in some than in others? In my field, everybody has a leak incidence but it varies. A middle range of leaks is the norm. Twenty-five to 35 per cent leaks is an unreasonable level. Eighty-five per cent of surgeons, according to a study, knew about this. Feedback of such information can influence future results.

A teaching District Director of Public Health has a different view.

Surgeons are almost entirely concerned with survival until discharge. We don't measure outcomes. We don't pursue death and complications to the point of personal responsibility. We only pursue this for educational purposes. We don't collect, analyse and feed back information on poor outcomes; we don't investigate in any depth. If the same consultant comes up [in complaints] more than once, we get more information. We haven't insisted on knowing that thorough peer review is taking place.

Considerable comparative statistical work has been done in surgery to compare outcomes around Britain. A consultant surgeon knowledgeable about the Confidential Enquiry into Postoperative Deaths (CEPOD) states:

You can tell a great deal about individual surgeons by looking at distribution curves. You feed the knowledge to them and they will improve. CEPOD is trying to pick the lowest 20 per cent of surgeons [concerning leak and infection rates] in the country. They range from 3 to 30 per cent. Those with 30 per cent rates changed and improved. Statistical information can make a difference.

These contradictory perceptions of more rigorous ways of judging competence that a few of those interviewed are thinking about hint at emerging new standards, the use of which remains marginal. Their marginality is captured in a statement by a retired professor of surgery:

> The technical side of medicine gets better and better and you can make fewer mistakes. We have to stop fumbling around. Medicine is *not* an art; the science is there. A lot of uncertainty could be resolved if we were more willing to accept scientific and rational approaches. We pay lip-service to science in our work but we don't use the proper tools of science in our work. Very many mistakes are avoidable if you apply the knowledge you have at your disposal. They are 'unavoidable' if you don't have the information. Our training doesn't include getting the 'buggers' out of our system. We don't emphasize professionalism right from the start.

But this is not the predominant view. It is a view that is growing as more people and institutions involved with health-care delivery challenge the ways in which the profession thinks about its work and its mishaps – indeed, how it has regulated itself in this area. The growing studies of medical outcomes, the growing research on medical errors conducted in collaboration between doctors and evaluation experts, and similar efforts are encouraging a fresh look at medical work and self-regulation, what it accomplishes and how it can be strengthened. This research will be reviewed in Chapter 6.

The predominant view remains strongly influenced by the previously mentioned seven overarching themes: uncertainty; fallibility; shared vulnerability; understanding and forgiveness; non-criticism; egregious errors; and professional judgement. Is this reality or is this indulgence? Does it reflect the current conditions of all medical practice or is it an increasingly outmoded professional self-perception of medical work?

Whichever. Given that these remain the dominant ways doctors seem to think about their work, it is easier to understand how these doctors respond to problems as they are revealed in work settings like the NHS hospitals and among GPs. How does information about problems spread? When do colleagues act on such information? And, most important, what do they attempt to do, informally, when confronted by a faltering colleague?

3

FRIENDLY EFFORTS:
THE INFORMAL MECHANISMS

Problems go on for a very long time. Other GPs may be suspicious but
they don't want to delve too deeply because if they know too much, they
will have to take action. So the problem may go on a very long time. It has
to be absolutely catastrophic and threatening patient harm for someone to
interfere.

(Regional general practice adviser)

The moment you become a consultant in [Britain], you are omni-
competent. You don't have to pay attention to your colleagues; you don't
have to pay attention to anybody.

(Emeritus professor of surgery)

THE WORLD OF THE GENERAL PRACTITIONER

British GPs are independent contractors to the NHS, unlike hospital doctors who are salaried employees of the Service. The independent status of the GPs is the seminal feature that characterizes the
traditional ethos of these important doctors: a strong sense of
clinical and professional autonomy. Like most of Europe's medical
professions, Britain's is sharply divided between the GP, who has
no hospital privileges, and the specialist. The GP is the gatekeeper
to the hospital specialist.

From the establishment of the Royal College of General Practitioners (RCGP) in the 1950s, the Doctor's Charter of 1966 and the
mandatory GPs' Vocational Training Act in the 1980s, professional
standards have risen dramatically but still remain an issue.
Although only a minority of GPs are members or fellows of the
College, it has contributed greatly to improving the quality of

medical practice. The Doctor's Charter improved general working conditions and the Training Act implemented rigorous educational standards. These have provided the building blocks to the new demands put on GPs in their NHS contracts in the 1990s. These contracts emphasize a number of new or enhanced quality assurance mechanisms including a preliminary form of medical audit.

The professional life of the GP is carried out in private offices and is buttressed by a variety of organizations that both support and constrain that work. NHS contracts are administered by the Family Health Service Authorities who oversee terms of contracts and contractual complaints. The Community Health Councils help patients with complaints. The Local Medical Committees, branches of the British Medical Association (BMA), expedite the professional interests of GPs, whether in solo, group or health centre practices. The BMA represents GPs nationally, including negotiations with the government over the terms of their contracts. The RCGP is concerned with educational standards. The General Medical Council maintains the Registry of all doctors and has the power to review complaints and discipline practitioners. This has focused primarily on GPs.[1] The Department of Health has monitored GP prescribing practices (now a responsibility of the new FHSAs) and other quality questions. In 1991, there were 27,888 GPs, with an average patient list size of 1,946.[2]

THE WORLD OF THE CONSULTANT SURGEON

Becoming a consultant in a British NHS hospital is a long and demanding process. The number of consultant posts is negotiated by the Department of Health and the appropriate royal college. They are limited, relative to the number of senior doctors in the hospitals, so the process of appointment is highly competitive. It is the top of the hospital professional ladder and is well compensated. Consultant surgeons, for example, will be among the best-compensated in a region. Consultants are fellows in their royal college, which requires passing a rigorous examination.

They can also have a private practice alongside their NHS employment. In addition, consultants may be awarded merit pay which not only increases their annual compensation but also affects their pensions. Consultant NHS contracts are for life. Current changes in the NHS may well impact on this latter condition. Trust hospitals can, theoretically, sign consultant contracts for as long or short a time as they wish. This is not yet happening, although trust short-term contracts for specific tasks have been noted. For the time being, life contracts remain a fact of consultant life in the NHS. According to the most recent available official statistics, there were 13,865 full-time-equivalent consultants and Senior House Medical Officers (SHMOs) on NHS hospital medical staff; of these, 3,874 were in surgical specialties.[3]

FINDING OUT ABOUT A PROBLEM

Senior GPs spend most of their time with patients, practice personnel and perhaps their partners if they schedule regular meetings. As they go about their routines, consultant surgeons are extremely busy and narrowly focused. Their work is carried out with the assistance of operating room nurses and junior doctors.

Managers are locked into their daily tasks but the nature of their work puts them in touch with many others. LMC secretaries, CHC secretaries and FHSA officers sit in the middle of information sources about problem doctors as part of their formal responsibilities.

Talk, gossip and rumours about colleagues are exchanged as in any work setting. The ways in which rumours, assessments and information about problem doctors reach colleagues, managers and relevant organizations is highly varied, related to work and friendship networks, interpersonal relationships and work style. There are abundant sources of information. They are, however, highly segmented. What is more problematic is how to judge the accuracy of the information and then, if anything, what to do about it.

Finding out about problem general practitioners

Information from inside the practice

> You learn a lot from the out-of-hours rota. You could tell from reading the record the next day, how your partner or an outside GP on the rota treated your patient. If he botched, you'd really be mad.
>
> (Senior GP partner, retired)

> There was a case where the GP was on barbiturates. The patients noticed she wasn't right in clinic and told a partner.
>
> (LMC secretary)

This [the GP not providing quality of service] is very difficult to establish since the contacts between doctor and patient are very private.

(Senior GP partner)

There is a danger of acting too quickly on the basis of these rumours. I'm often hearing of doctors who are falsely accused.

(Regional GP adviser)

Information from outside the practice

This job as LMC secretary throws up a large number of problems. Some can be dealt with and some can't. Because of my personal contact with the GPs, they ask me about everything.

As CHC secretary, I have periodic meetings with the FHSA and we exchange informal information [about GPs]. We also have an exchange of information between the CHC and friendly consultants.

This CHC began to identify 'multiple complaint' doctors as we heard from patients, families, other GPs and consultants, particularly the 'heavyweight' consultants.

The FHSA begins to note which doctors, for whom they manage contracts, are suspicious. As FHSA manager I have noted an increase in the dissolution of GP partnerships, a noticeably increasing incidence. Maybe the increase is because . . . juniors are disappointed in seniors' standards . . . or, bad doctors are being pushed out. They move to another area and go into single-handed practice where they can get away with catastrophe, can't be detected, nobody knows.

Professors in charge of vocational training posts for GPs hear from students about questionable behaviour.

There is a tendency for local people to be coy about the subject of competence. The LMC tends to act as a protective trade union. The LMC (and the FHSA), after all, actually have no authority to deal with competence. Their only sanction is to report to the GMC, which they are very hesitant to do.

(GP regional adviser)

These rumours . . . there is a great difficulty if you don't know the full circumstances. There is a question of natural justice. Often this is hearsay evidence which a GP can't answer. That isn't right. Then there is reluctance on the part of partners to send forth a complaint. Hard to get concrete evidence.

(Regional GP Adviser)

Doctors don't know how to say 'Help'. They are trained not to admit incompetence. GPs are not good at confronting a colleague. And those who are incompetent isolate themselves.

(Former Department of Health GP Regional Medical Officer)

There are many who assess the GPs

It is surprising to realize just how many local and national organizations have access to information about the clinical and professional behaviour of GPs. There are the Local Medical Committee secretaries and chairs, the FHSA secretaries and chairs, the Community Health Council secretaries and the former Department of Health GP Regional Directors of Public Health.

Local Medical Committees: the GPs' trade union

As LMC secretary I am a GP to the GPs, looking after the welfare [of over 1,000 of them]. My job is to see things from the GPs' point of view. I know at least half by name. This job as LMC secretary throws up a large number of problems. Some can be dealt with and some can't. Because of my personal contact with the GPs, they ask me about everything: getting a partner, new premises, complaints. Usually they ring me up to do a service for them. Sooner or later, if they have to deal with a complaint at the Medical Services Committee (MSC) they ask me to go with them. Alcohol and retirement issues come to me in three ways: a colleague or partner notices the illness, unofficially through the Family Health Services Authority (FHSA) but this doesn't happen too often, or, through my own observation.

   The FHSA has a statutory duty to do something if a doctor is ill. They can disbar him but this is rare. Of the 1,200 doctors, I worry about perhaps 12–15. I'm worried about incompetence, about inefficiency, about fraudulence. Doctors find it so difficult to deal with these things; they are just not trained to deal with them. But they can shovel them off on me. I am objective and fair and I have to protect the doctors from themselves.

Information from the Family Health Services Authorities

This woman has been in her new job as co-manager of a large city FHSA for only six weeks. She is outspoken and aggressive, looking forward to the reforms that will strengthen the managers and provide them with new tools, more discretion in using the FHSA resources and new powers to inspect and close bad GP premises. She says she has no confidence in professional self-regulation.

> The GPs currently on the FHSA-MSC go to extremes acting on behalf of the GPs. Our experience here is that the patients go out extremely dissatisfied, feeling that the MSC proceedings are stacked against them, and they are. The way the contracts are written totally protects the doctor. The majority of the complaints about competence turn into court cases but it has to be a way-out error because the public hasn't enough knowledge to know an error. We can tell you the incompetents . . . probably 10 per cent of our GPs: they're very elderly and they are impaired. They are single-handed but so are some of the best doctors. A badly incompetent doctor, not ill, is totally impossible. It's almost impossible to force a resignation. We did do one and it is now in the hands of a solicitor who is claiming the doctor is *not* sick. His GP won't sign anything. And I personally have no confidence that a clinically incompetent doctor will ever be removed from practice by the new medical audit system. It just has to be horrendous for anything to happen.
>   It's too hard for them to face. But the new FHSA will have leverage to do something about the incompetent and the rude GP, something they lack the ability to do now.

Role of the Community Health Councils

The CHCs, a unique feature of the NHS, were established in the NHS reorganization of 1982. Their job is to help consumers with their complaints and foster health education. The CHCs must be consulted by the District Health Authorities about any proposed closures in the district. They operate on small annual budgets from the NHS.

A young CHC secretary says:

> Over the years, I've got in my head that there are three categories of GPs: those that are really very good, perhaps 20 per cent; the 70 per cent that are middling and avoid trouble; and the definitely unsatisfactory from a clinical point of view – about 10 per cent.

How did he determine this? Some information he got from his predecessor. Much also comes from patient complaints and how doctors respond:

> I will have seen how the GPs responded to previous complaints. I'm more impressed with a GP who responds with full details, who knows what happened as opposed to the scribbled note: 'This is a difficult patient.'

This CHC secretary goes on to say that a great deal of information comes from two surveys of GPs he conducted when he first started, one inquiring about hours, languages spoken, age and sex of GPs, any special services offered, public transport, and so on. For the 20 they could not reach, office visits were made and impressions formed.

A second survey was done of members of the primary health-care team: home helps, social workers, district nurses, health visitors, where they were asked what they thought of the GPs. He also found that *ad hoc* contact with team members at social events and conferences provided information, usually expressed in a circumspect fashion. A district nurse might say, 'This GP should get his cataracts fixed so he can identify jaundice', something that could never be said formally because she had to continue working with the GP.

Two other CHC secretaries also emphasized informal networks of information, aside from the patient complaint as a source. One experienced CHC secretary had cultivated a group of consultants and GPs, generally the 'best' doctors, on whom he could rely, and whom he occasionally met at a pub for a drink. Another secretary also had a coterie of consultants who could be called on for information and for help, but she relied primarily on midwives, nurses, health visitors and social workers for information.

All the secretaries report an informal relationship with the LMCs, FHSAs and health authorities. There is a good deal of telephone contact, exchange of information and making queries about particular doctors. Two of them developed good consultant and GP contacts, people with whom they could check information and from whom patients might get help and encouragement to go to the CHC with their complaints.

Former Department of Health GP Regional Medical Officers

There was a powerful source of information about GPs carried to the Department of Health and shared, on the district level, with FHSA officials and sometimes with LMCs: the Department of Health GP Regional Medical Officers. While these positions ceased to exist in 1991, information from this source is revealing of how problem doctors could be identified.

The major task of the RMOs was to review GP prescribing patterns. While carrying out that job, which saw them visiting 600–800 GPs a year (in three-year cycles), they also were required to ask a number of questions about all aspects of the practice work. Some of this information was then shared with FHSAs ('we matched our lists'), LMCs and others concerned with GP standards. These functions have now been transferred to the FHSAs.

One experienced Department of Health RMO summed up what all the D of H RMOs had to say. He listed the signs of trouble, in addition to unusual prescribing patterns: a sudden break-up of a partnership, reduction of list size in an area with population growth, difficulty arranging home visits, poor management skills, premises in bad condition, signing off excessively on sickness benefit forms. However, it could take some years to build up a convincing picture of problems – perhaps, this D of H RMO suggested, as long as five years.

> Problems could go on for years until something goes horribly wrong. Then it comes out that people knew for years that there were problems but just preferred not to act. Who will do the talking to the GP? Remember that GPs are in competition with each other for patients. It's usually a neighbouring GP who talks to him and the bloke will think: 'He just wants to get my patients.' There could be a conspiracy of silence; colleagues and patients willing to put up with a lot, willing to forgive.
>
> What really complicates these problems is how fiercely independent GPs are. And so there is this failure to approach the problems until the situation becomes impossibly bad.

People were covering up. If things were really bad, there might be a frank talk. If it were an elderly GP, they would try to get him to retire early. I recall an alcoholic GP. Can an alcoholic be a good doctor? That's nonsense; he can't be good. This single-handed GP had given terrific service for 25–30 years. During the war, he gave heroic service to the community. But he drank heavily and, in the last ten years, showed signs of being an alcoholic. His practice was in a remote area and he did surgeries in different places. Everyone knew he stopped at the top of the hill for a stiff whisky. So patients with big problems would catch him there before he took that drink. You know the definition of an alcoholic? It's someone who drinks more than their doctor.

He continued:

There are few totally incompetent GPs around, more marginally incompetent. I'd say, in my area, 10 per cent are a worry and 1 per cent are dangerous. It is either their state of mind, or their health, or they just can't meet the demands of their practice. A few are downright dangerous and about 50 per cent of those are single-handed.

The FHSAs know about the bad doctors by virtue of the complaints. They may share it with the LMC secretaries as a last resort. I've sat on an LMC; they really don't know; they don't want to know. And the CHC is low on the list because of the small number of people who come to it.

Finding out about problem consultants

Inside consultant circles:

You don't realize how hard consultants in the NHS work. So you only get the grossest of ideas of what your colleagues are doing.

We don't watch each other operate but, as regional adviser [for the Royal College of Surgeons] I hear from the anaesthesiologists; they are the most important sources of information. Junior doctors might chatter or hint about a problem, and senior nurses, using very circumspect language. I might seek information, indirectly, from the Senior Registrar. Only occasionally do others come to me.

As the medical general manager, I saw all complaints. I heard from patients, colleagues, other consultants in other fields, junior doctors. The intrinsic difficulty is sorting out actual incompetence. At lunch we gossip and say things that are quite untrue. People get 'blacked' by their colleagues because of personality. But one gets an inkling. One of the surgeons sends me patients where everything seems bungled. I'd never refer a patient to him.

There is always the problem of how to prove hearsay. There are corridor conversations. There are rumours planted to deliberately discredit a fellow consultant. These all have to be treated cautiously. You'd hear all this gossip over lunch and feel helpless about what could be done. I'd just make sure my patients never got in those doctors' wards.

As a consultant I can tell you that it might take for ever for a general manager to know about incompetence. Only people working here know right away. Then it's very difficult to know what to do.

Outside consultant circles

As DDPH of this area, I meet informally with the chair of the medical staff council and we discuss rumours or concerns about doctors. The chair will make informal enquiries and they set out a plan of action.

Since I have been District Nursing Officer, I do a periodic walk around. I visit many of the wards. Individual nurses might pass remarks. The nurses will speak to the nurse manager who talks to the surgeon. It would probably take a trained nurse a year to confirm incompetence in the operating theatre. Nurses have hunches, they work at the emotional level; they'll be hesitant to pass judgement. But I hear from the Director of Nursing about an incorrect prescription, always being late to clinic, late on ward rounds, the time it takes to perform surgery, drink on duty. They only report it after it happens several times. Something major they report immediately. I go to the District Director of Public Health only with facts. Then the DDPH and I go to the chair of the Medical Staff Committee only when we have a great concern. The chair might indicate with a nod and a wink that he already knows. It would be my expectation that the chair would talk to the doctor.

As a new hospital manager, it took two years before I got into the informal information networks but I had information immediately from my review of legal claims. Also, I've observed doctors are constantly gossiping about each other in the consultants' dining room until the person arrives. The doctors are incredibly critical of each other – really lash out. I wonder what their standards of information are about each other's competence when I see what the doctors' standards are for facts about administrative issues. I take some of the banter seriously; it depends on who is saying it. Then I would go to a very senior consultant. But I feel a great deal of confidence about an approach like the Three Wise Men. I trust the Three Wise Men.

According to the Community Health Council secretaries, some doctors, unable to confront their problem colleagues, see that knowledge of incompetence or problems get into the system through the CHCs. Here are some views:

The heavyweights, the best of the doctors, have cultivated the CHCs. This CHC has contact with some of the best consultants in the region and they send patients with serious complaints to us.

GPs make judgements from the case notes that discharge letters contain. Are they thorough? Are they hastily written? With a consultant who is losing skills this may be noticed by the GPs. Then the consultant will be serving a low number of patients. There won't be a waiting list.

(Senior GP)

GP trainees doing hospital attachments can spot incompetence.

(Regional GP adviser)

A former Regional Director of Public Health rattles off a long list of information sources.

I had a sherry hour in my office where people dropped by on their way home. I saw things myself; I heard from consultants' secretaries, from operating room staff, from nurses; from other consultants, general practitioners, junior doctors in training, who would be very cautious and circumspect in their wording; from lay people responding to the Department of Health Circular on *Prevention of Harm to Patients*.

Another RDPH says:

> I get out and about as much as possible. I have an amazing
> number of contacts since I've been around so long. Consultants
> ring me up, lay chairs will ring me up, I'm in close touch with
> the DGM and DDPH. The BMA and the defence societies sort
> things out on the phone. There may be a case of a 'conspiracy'
> between me and the Medical Defence Union about a specific
> case. My most important sources of information are the
> District General Manager, the Three Wise Men and telephone
> calls from individuals. Consultants can judge, within three
> months, the winners from the average. I'm not at all satisfied
> with my information sources. When I'm brought in, I realize
> that things have gone quite far. I should have come in earlier.
> We can be talking about years before matters reach me. There
> is a fear that to report to me is likely to lead to the end of a
> career rather than rehabilitation.

One new RDPH, during a briefing by his predecessor, was
asked:

> 'Would you like a list of consultants in the region who are a
> problem?' He then produced a six-page list of people who
> might or might not become problems. Only a few got worse. It
> was tremendously helpful. Of course, regional meetings put
> me in touch with information networks on a weekly basis, for
> example, with managers. I think the hospital grapevine is 98
> per cent accurate.

However, a DDPH in a non-teaching district says:

> I get very little information about these things. It's often
> fortuitous, usually informal at meetings, from nurses or
> consultants or GPs. Never from the FHSA or CHC.

A summary of information sources is given in Table 3.1

DISCUSSION ON INFORMATION SOURCES

Six elements stand out in thinking about the process of 'finding out'
about problem doctors. First, the sources of information are more
extensive than might appear on the surface. But, second, there is no
mechanism for centralized sharing other than personal contacts
between people who meet at work or play. The information is in

Table 3.1 Sources of information

	General practitioners	*Consultant surgeons*
Inside	Patients Juniors Out-of-hours rota Partner's personal observation	Anaesthesiologists Juniors Operating theatre nurses

Outside	FHSA
	CHCs
	LMC secretaries
	Consultants
	Chemists
	Vocational trainees
	Old Department of Health
	  RDPHs
	Other members of primary care
	  team
		Referral doctors
		Patients
		GPs
		Managers at
		  many levels
		CHCs

fragments, scattered throughout the hospital, district or region. Some individuals, by the nature of their job responsibilities, are accumulating 'files'. Some will be discarded and some will build. Third, one's interpersonal style and role in a particular region or district influences access to information. Fourth, there is the challenge of differentiating facts from hearsay. Fifth, there is confusion about who has responsibility and for what. For this and reasons of professional reticence, and the knowledge that any informal disciplinary efforts will be arduous, time-consuming and uncomfortable, it can, finally, be a long time before even the first informal remedial steps are taken.

A number of contradictory perceptions are evident. Some consultants think every consultant is too busy to know what goes on with other consultants; some consultants make it their business to know what is going on or get such hints because of their status. Some of the 'best' consultants appear to steer injured patients to the local Community Health Councils. Some consultants seem to think that managers 'haven't a clue', yet managers appear to have a good number of sources of information. Their problem is inability to make a judgement on clinical matters. The two big issues are how to assess the information or rumours and who should do what.

CONFRONTED WITH A PROBLEM COLLEAGUE

Once someone with responsibility or someone who cares is satisfied that there is a problem, what are the informal steps such a person can begin to take? The anecdotes already discussed and others to come reveal a small repertoire of informal mechanisms that colleagues and professional organizations employ.

Three distinct informal mechanisms emerge from an analysis of the anecdotal cases for both GPs and consultants: The *quiet chat* (personal persuasion); *protective support*; and *work shifting* and *diverting patient flow*. There are also two quasi-informal mechanisms: being *pushed out of the partnership*; and *the Three Wise Men*.

The quiet chat: personal persuasion

In the hospital, when the signs of some sort of problem or incompetence are sufficiently confirmed, the chair of the Medical Executive Committee, along with close collegial friends of the doctor in question, will initiate a series of quiet, informal approaches, described by some interviewees as 'little stick' and 'big stick' talks, or the 'terribly quiet chat'. In some private moment, perhaps at the pub or bar, sometimes in a social setting, the aim is to let the doctor know there are concerns and suspicions, to get some sense of self-awareness, more information and, if appropriate, begin a process of persuasion to change the offensive behaviour.

Among GPs, the LMC secretary or LMC chair (both general practitioners) may initiate the talk. Or a close colleague may be persuaded to do it. Perhaps the FHSA secretary and the CHC secretary will be included, depending on work relationships between these groups.

The 'talking to' is predicated on the assumption that it is possible to persuade the doctor to change behaviour. The 'little stick' talk conveys friendly concern about inappropriate behaviour and alerts the doctor that such behaviour has come to colleagues' attention. The 'big stick' talk suggests stronger action. If change does not occur, there is a veiled threat that much stronger action will be taken – perhaps a manager or the Royal College will be brought into the scene. Sometimes the talk works; sometimes not.

In this case, a colleague and an administrator work together.

Three and a half years ago we brought in a new cardiothoracic surgeon – young, competent, lots of internationally recognized work on trauma. He began at a great pace. He was brought in to build up a cardiac unit. Like many of his type, his nature was bombastic, self-promoting, thrusting to the extreme. He was exceptionally determined to have his own way. He caused upsets but was doing extremely good work. The publicity he received was good; he manipulated the media to perpetuate his national and international reputation, to an extent that he alienated many doctors and nurses. My concern was that he suffered delusionary tendencies. I believe he sold stories to the newspapers, courted TV and got coverage. The Royal College of Surgeons was getting anxious about him to such a degree, we thought we had to do something about it.

He was talked to on many occasions by the professor of surgery. He would behave for a week and then fall back. I had enough evidence (statements from nurses, newspaper material) so around Christmas, with the professor of surgery who was very strong, we set in motion a strategy. We decided, for his own career prospects, that the professor and I would have an hour with him. That seems to have worked; he has changed his behaviour.

Had that not worked, he would have been seen by the chair of the Medical Staff Council; we would have brought in the Three Wise Men but prior to that, we would have asked him to interview with the professor of psychiatry. I had evidence that in his talks, he was ignoring mortality and morbidity statistics. He was boosting his ego; it was delusionary. There is a fear of being seen by the Three Wise Men. This would be known internally and nationally.

The following case was described by a senior hospital consultant surgeon.

This case concerns a consultant in another specialty where I know quite a lot. He was of some 12–14 years' standing as a consultant. He was perceived first by his junior and nursing staff as making some unusual management decisions. The junior house officers gossiped that he was making patient management decisions that in their eyes were of questionable standard. At that stage, other consultants were not aware of it. There was no reason for other consultants to see his patients. It was perhaps a year or eighteen months when word got back to them. By the odd hint, mentioned over beer, the consultants became aware that this consultant was making some strange decisions, possibly something was not quite right. Some informed soundings were made. There was a quiet chat with him where they said they had heard some questions asked. They felt it only right he should know this unfortunate gossip at the junior doctor/nurse level. Would he like to discuss it? Perhaps change in the future?

He would not accept that his standards were inadequate. He was amazed to hear it. There was no justification. He wouldn't accept that there was any problem but he would look into the matter. It was hoped the problem would fade away but it didn't settle. The next thing was that in rearranging the junior staff rota, one junior said he wouldn't work with this consultant; he felt he would resign first. The medical executive committee decided to invoke the Three Wise Men. They had a series of interviews with the consultant, juniors and nurses. The consultant was asked if he would undergo a medical exam, which took place. He was found to be normal.

He continued to deny mismanagement and could see no justifiable criticism. He maintained that the reasons for the complaints were on a personality basis and accepted there had been personality problems. The juniors and nurses agreed there were personality problems but said that the real problem was his management. Administration knew the enquiry was in progress and had full access to what was going on, to all documents right along. The health authority looked at the matter. Its chair interviewed the consultant. There was a series of meetings with the chair and the consultant without any satisfactory outcome. The consultant still maintained he was managing on a satisfactory level. Others disagreed. Some of his decisions were highly unconventional and arguably dangerous.

The case came to an impasse. He kept maintaining it was a personality problem and said: 'Prove to me what I did was incompetent.' It didn't go to enquiry but he was offered early retirement which he declined on grounds that if he accepted, it was tantamount to admitting guilt. The consultant has been suspended by the health authority for two years now. The consultant's appeal is in progress. There has been a whole series of legal discussions. The consultant is now doing locum work as a GP in the region. This case shows how difficult it is to get anyone to change. Things are quite difficult.

A clinical director of surgery described another case:

[The] case involved a radiologist who left the screen on too long. This was noticed by the radiographers who told the other radiologists. They put it to her that she was using too much. This technique was very effective.

There was one surgeon where the nurses always knew that his patients would have infections. The ward nurses said they must have been acquired in the theatre. They were traced back to the theatre and to this surgeon. It was reported to the Medical Staff Committee and the senior surgeon spoke to the chap, privately, behind closed doors so the nurses wouldn't know. The surgeon had to face his problems and things improved. Usually there is very much a collusion between the theatre nurse and surgeon unless there are poor relations. How far a nurse will go depends on the nurse's own integrity. I never heard a nurse say: 'I can't stand working with that chap.' They protest with their feet, by leaving, but it's hard to pin this down.

A consultant surgeon described an alcoholism case that was resolved in the department by the chair.

The junior staff commented about their concern. One or two of us observed him for a few months. All this happened over a year's period. The chair talked privately to him and his wife. He was within five years of retirement. He was able to control his problem and retired at the normal retirement age.

The chair of an LMC described a GP taking barbiturates:

The patients noticed that she wasn't right in clinic and a partner contacted me. I went [to see her] and challenged her: 'What are you on?' Her husband went with me and we found drugs in her purse. The next step was that she suspended herself from duty. We got a psychiatrist to see her and take her on. She came back to practise and lapsed again. Then she left the district and went elsewhere as a locum. She was picked up by the police for odd behaviour and I was contacted to keep her out of the courts. She was brought to the GMC and lost her right to prescribe. Then we got her a job doing pathology in a district hospital.

When the RDPH has charge of the problem, he has a version of the 'talk' as well:

Discussion is the key feature. Talks and working out a reasonable experience for the doctor involved. I always talk directly to the consultant. 'I understand you are having a problem of——. Can you tell me about it?' We talk at length. I talk to others: senior colleagues, administrators, other medical officers, my personnel section staff. I try to build up a picture of the situation. Nine times out of ten, the personnel officer at the regional health authority knows about everyone.

I'm trying to work out whether the story is factually correct. My serious concern is with the possibility of malice for personal reasons. A lot of malice is going on. If it is malice, I don't want to be involved. Maybe one in ten cases is malice. In ten years there was only one case that was completely malice.

Protective support: the gentlemanly approach

In certain cases, the group around the difficult doctor will have developed a system of 'protective support'. That is, in a gradually evolving act of friendly collusion, colleagues, junior doctors and nurses quietly shift work away from the doctor and do it for him. In this way, patients are protected from the doctor and the doctor is protected from himself. In some reported cases, protective support is carried on for several years until it becomes too much of a burden or the difficult doctor simply becomes too difficult to handle in this manner. Occasionally the doctor is protected until retirement.

A consultant in his forties had a series of personal illnesses which undoubtedly could have affected his physical and mental ability to work. He was a popular doctor and his colleagues carried him for several years – very able senior and junior colleagues. They did much of his clinical work. Then there was a very definite deterioration and I was alerted by his colleagues. But I had been aware of his illness because he was off sick and I was aware of his state through personal contact. From the beginning, I asked the colleagues: 'How is it going? Everything OK?' They said 'Yes, we are coping.' We had explicit discussions: will he harm patients? I was assured no, he wouldn't harm patients.

All district consultants elect a chair of the medical staff council; this is their top representative. I meet with him, informally, every two weeks. Any rumours or concerns like this I discuss with him. From this discussion, the chair can make very informal enquiries. I can get back to him next time if things are not as I had been assured and we will plan some action.

The prognosis for the young doctor was poor and there was a recurrence of his illness. When I got more anxious, I spoke directly with the young consultant. He was sure he was all right. There were no complaints and he was keen to continue working. But when there was even further deterioration, we

went to the Three Wise Men. Two outside consultants were
invited to look at the records and interview him. It was decided
that he should retire early on medical grounds with an
enhanced pension, and this happened. He died one or two
years after early retirement.

The doctors were able to ease their conscience *vis-à-vis* their
colleague; his children were now older. We didn't collect
outcome data; no quizzing; it was a gentlemanly approach.
Had he been a surgeon, theoretically the process would have
been speeded up, but in [Britain], I doubt it.

(District Director of Public Health)

This business of protection – yes, it's used where there are
questions of health, alcoholism, physical health even more, but
not if it goes too far. These are not strictly competence cases. I
remember the case of the blind doctor. Six months of blindness
was covered so carefully. People who are part of the team
operate quickly for the team. But, if there is a sudden
deterioration of the condition, the crowd offering protection
lose their nerve; they can't protect the patients any more.
There was an Accident and Emergency consultant whose
vision was deteriorating. His colleagues treated and protected
him. Now, they suddenly realize that his vision is so bad, that
they can't let him continue to work. It went to the Three Wise
Men and then to the administration. You know, sometimes I
ring up the chief of the medical staff to get the Three Wise Men
going. All the RDPHs can do this. There is also a national
scheme for sick doctors. But it has two drawbacks. It tries too
hard to remain aloof from administration. And, if an offer of
help is rejected, it does nothing more.

(Regional Director of Public Health)

A physician was caught by the police for drunk driving. My
office received the court transcription. I spoke with the
consultant. I spoke with his peer group and said it was their
duty to let me know about these things. I asked the nurses to
enquire about the number of times he's turned up with alcohol
on his breath; if there were any cancellations of ward rounds or
clinic. They were reassuring. It's important to rely on some
support from colleagues. If this had been a life or death
situation, I don't know what we would have done. I suppose
first, protect the colleague, second, protect the patient, third,
protect the good name of the district health authority.

(District Director of Public Health)

We had an anaesthesiologist who had problems at forty. He became epileptic. He was allowed to work as long as he had a colleague with him in the theatre. This went on for a year. At the end of that time he continued to have fits. He couldn't practise on his own. He was given early retirement.

(District Director of Public Health)

Nurses tell me that surgeons, if they make a mistake, expect loyalty, even collusion. If the relationship is not too good from the beginning this will break down quickly. But there are many ways theatre nurses protect doctors. They say during an operation: 'Have you forgotten this? This? Would you like to do this? This?' But you do hear nurses say: 'I wouldn't have that doctor take care of me. He's knife-happy.' If a nurse finds a doctor doing things wrong all the time she'll speak to her nursing manager who will talk to the surgeon. If she's respected as a theatre manager they will listen. On balance, people are left to do their own thing and doctors don't criticize outside their own specialty.

(District Nursing Officer)

We had one problem in this district that was due to illness. A surgeon had three cardiac arrests and suffered cerebral damage. The region let him continue. We [in the department] said 'No' and aborted his appointment. The immediate problem was his doing cardiac surgery. The Regional Director of Public Health got an independent medical opinion who was unable to make a decision. The RDPH found it a difficult case on the evidence presented. He was allowed to come back. The man accused was colourful and extroverted. Even when he was well, he was a difficult colleague. If he had had a more normal personality, he might have been quietly rehabilitated. We were bailing out the problems in the background. His insight was not right. We invoked the Three Wise Men who asked the RDPH to reconsider since his colleagues wouldn't accept him. He was 53. He died ten years later after being employed as a surgeon locum.

(Consultant surgeon, district hospital)

Diverting patient flow

One element of 'protective support' emerges as a mechanism by itself: diverting the patient flow, but without full protective support. This can be carried out by the nurse or receptionist who handles patient appointments, for example. It can also be done by a number of doctors who simply stop referring to a particular specialist. For example, GPs in a district may decide a particular surgeon is no longer performing to a certain standard. Or, a group of surgeons may decide a particular radiologist is no longer to be trusted to provide accurate information about their patients. An internist makes sure certain surgeons do not take care of his patients. A consultant surgeon says:

> It's typical among consultant teams to do a number of things. They would talk to local GPs and tell them not to refer to this consultant. Other consultants would not refer. You'd tell juniors working with this consultant to call upon you if something happens.

A District Nursing Officer related how

> nurses would discover so-and-so is on call. They would just not bother to call him because of his incompetence. They would wait until the morning shift. Or they may call Dr. A with whom there is an informal agreement to do something in order to take care of the patient.

A consultant oncologist says:

> It is difficult to affect the flow of patients if there are only a limited number of consultants. You can only control them a bit. There is an X-ray consultant here and the consultants doubt his ability. But he gives extra good service to the GPs so he gets a lot of work from them.

The information gathered by CHC secretaries is also used in other, more direct ways to divert patients. When people ask the CHC for names of GPs whose list they might join, those about whom there have been suspicious stories or actual complaints may not appear on the list. 'There are certain names I've never given to anyone.'

QUASI-FORMAL MECHANISMS: THE PROFESSIONAL GROUP TAKES ACTION

Groups of professionals, confronted with problem doctors, may take action in more formal ways. The GPs in a partnership may change the composition of the partnership. The chief of the

Hospital Medical Council, with other senior consultants, may institute a quiet internal review known as the Three Wise Men (TWM). There is also a local GP Three Wise Men protocol. A royal college may be brought in to scrutinize a training programme or assist with a problem. The BMA has a special ethics committee that is available to offer advice.

Pushed out of the partnership

General practitioner partnerships are relationships typically based on legal arrangements between partners. There is also a contract between the GP partners or solo practitioner and the FHSA to provide services for the NHS. Under unusual circumstances a partnership may break up, one partner asked to leave or leaving unilaterally. If the GP who leaves is a 'problem' doctor, one of the consequences of the change may be that the doctor is pushed into more isolation where there are even fewer opportunities for outside observation.

A GP academic describes a case of partnership change.

The structure of general practice and partnerships in the UK makes this whole area complex and this is illustrated when you deal with these problems [of competence]. It was apparent in a practice for some years that one GP was not pulling his weight, not sharing the burdens of the practice. It was suspected that he was not providing quality of service. This is very difficult to establish since the contacts between doctor and patient are very private, but there was a suspicion for some time.

A problem surfaced when one or two patients made comments about what a long time it was taking to get appointments with a specialist consultant. When investigating this, it was found that the letters to the specialists had not been written. This provided hard information that could be taken up with the GP. It was discussed and he said he'd forgotten all about it, he'd been so busy. We said: 'You must pull your socks up. This brings us all into bad repute.' The problem got more serious when we discovered, in fact, that false documentation had been entered into the record in a referral he made.

The partners decided to take action and said to him: 'This behaviour is not acceptable in our practice.' He would have to leave the practice. This happened after advice from lawyers, the GMC, the defence society. This advice was necessary since it was impossible to establish that a patient had been harmed or that there was incompetence. People are not perfect; there are lapses. People can get away with incompetence without the professional machinery treating it seriously. We have to overcome our tendency not to interfere. The first concern is patient harm.

This individual left the practice but is now practising in a not-too-distant community. He's been able to attract patients. Patients obviously take sides.

How long were the problems going on? That's very difficult to say. A very long time. He had a more casual approach in these particular matters; he was competent as an average doctor in other ways. The professional organization's position is that some colleagues are too critical of others. This may or may not be true. Certainly one gets the feeling that professionals are protective of colleagues. 'There but for the grace of God . . .'. But as patients, it may not be very acceptable.

Hospital consultants and the Three Wise Men

In some hospital cases, if none of the informal mechanisms produce the desired results, the chair of the Medical Executive Committee will institute a Three Wise Men procedure. This may be regarded as a quasi-formal mechanism. It is unique to British hospitals. In 1964, the Department of Health and Social Services circulated a suggestion that the medical staff of NHS hospitals designate three highly respected consultants to serve as an informal investigative committee.[4] Typically it is doctors that initiate the Three Wise Men procedure, although a manager can request it as well.

They are to gather facts quietly, including a talk with the problem doctor, and then report and make recommendations to the chair as well as the District or Regional Director of Public Health, if desired and if the latter has been informed of the difficulties. Often they are not informed; this depends on the nature of their rapport with the medical staff. While the Department of Health Circular suggests that this committee should be activated informally in cases involving suspected impairment, it is clear from the cases that the Three Wise Men are invoked for more than suspected impairment. And there are mixed opinions about how effective the Three Wise Men are.

When it was clear the alcoholism was continuing, we set up a Three Wise Men procedure. The committee set-up was composed of the chair of the medical staff committee, the chair of the division concerned and the DDPH (me! that was unusual). We met; we talked to three of his colleagues; we all agreed that there was a case to answer; we were concerned about his competence. The chair of the Three Wise Men saw the consultant and he wisely accepted treatment. A report went to the RDPH. He stayed in treatment three months, guaranteed that he was dry and physically improved.

After discussion between his doctor, me, the RDPH, his colleagues, he came back to work. He's been back to work a year. I see him every two months. His performance is different. Perhaps he's not back to his old sharpness. But the problem now is his relationship with his colleagues. It's not back to its earlier harmony.

(District Director of Public Health)

A retired RDPH describes a variation of the Three Wise Men. In this RDPH's region, the Three Wise Men deal with three kinds of issues: contracts matters; health problems; and competence.

These are often intertwined. A colleague could deal with the problem directly or take it to the chair of the Three Wise Men which, in our region, was composed of the chair of the Medical Executive Committee, the chief of the Medical Staff Committee and the chair of the appropriate specialty department. Open protective support may be a solution suggested by the Three Wise Men and I think that it is effective and useful. In my experience, it has always been effective with health problems like drinking, drugs, mental and physical health. The Three Wise Men have discretion to report to the RDPH and might use this threat to pressure the 'errant one'.

It is an example of colleagues being corporatively protective. It's an internal enquiry whereby some decision is made to offer protective support. It's investigative rather than punitive and we are anxious to have Three Wise Men procedures. When I started this job I was rather surprised how little of this there was. Now there are probably four or five in one year. The Three Wise Men decide about protective support and get my approval. In one recent case, the protective support collapsed but we decided to reinstate it. I feel that patients are protected and the doctor is performing.

(Regional Director of Public Health)

A new manager in a teaching hospital sees the Three Wise Men as the most powerful consultants in the district.

Doctors do respond to the threat of invoking a Three Wise Men procedure. It is an effective tool; doctors themselves are effective in taking care of problem doctors.

Not everyone, including those who serve on it, is as positive about the use and effectiveness of the Three Wise Men. An emeritus professor of surgery says:

There was an alcoholic internist. He was regularly becoming incompetent in his daily duties and decision-making. We, the Three Wise Men, gathered circumstantial evidence. That's the nature of the evidence you are likely to get. We were able to act temporarily as he was prepared to admit that he wasn't doing too well. We had no method, as the Three Wise Men, to say: 'You must get treatment.' This doctor was in treatment but the problem repeated itself time and again. He is still practising.

A consultant surgeon suggests:

The Three Wise Men should adopt a more inquisitive role . . . get aggressive. Keep an eye on things rather than waiting for things to turn up. Take a more active role rather than waiting until someone comes to you.

A senior GP made the following observations:

It's unlikely that it's necessary to invoke the Three Wise Men. They are really a closing of the ranks. If mistakes are made in a hospital, my impression is that, if it comes to an enquiry, often the junior person involved gets the blame. Only when things are going really wrong do the Three Wise Men get invoked. It's like shutting the stable door after the horse has bolted as far as protection for patients is concerned.

Regional Directors of Public Health also disagree among themselves about the effectiveness of the Three Wise Men.

It doesn't work as well as it should. If you don't publicize it repeatedly no one knows it exists. The Three Wise Men have no training to do this job. It's too much a secret chamber. It may be difficult to recognize abnormal behaviour because it develops slowly, insidiously. It's difficult to take an objective, analytic look [at a colleague's behaviour]. Growing alcoholism gets labelled 'just his style'. Drugs change behaviour ever so slowly. And it is an invidious task. The doctor in question is most likely to reject that he has a problem. It's hard to communicate to the staff how it [the Three Wise Men procedure] works and new staff haven't a clue.

(Regional Director of Public Health)

The Three Wise Men don't work because consultants are all peers. There is no hierarchy. . . . Contrast that with nursing. Various levels of nursing managers can keep kicking the tough problems up to the highest nurse manager who is then removed enough to impose direct action. Equal peers can't do this to each other.

(District Director of Public Health)

A district nursing officer with extensive experience in a teaching hospital declares:

the idea of the Three Wise Men is good but it's awfully hard to get medical colleagues to condemn a doctor. I can't think of another way unless you have a medical director. Actually, consultants consist of eccentric individuals. They do things their own way and others are reluctant to criticize.

A consultant surgeon active in the Royal College expressed the following opinion:

The Three Wise Men are rarely effective on serious matters because consultants manipulate the Three Wise Men system. Perhaps they are effective with impaired-doctor issues and minor disciplinary issues but they are not effective when the issue is incompetence.

A consultant surgeon in a regional hospital said:

I was only aware of the Three Wise Men being used once. And there was a personality clash between the chair of the Three Wise Men and the doctor in question.

Nobody can be sure how well these procedures work because no records are kept, and no data published. However, they are widely perceived as ineffective by those who are interested in the problems of sick doctors. The 1975 Merrison Commission concluded that they were 'insufficiently effective' and 'not widely enough understood'.[5] Indeed, L. Pilowski relates the response of an administrator in the health authority to a request for the names of the 'Wise Men' by a surgical senior registrar worried about his alcoholic chief. 'Sorry, that is confidential', he was told.[6]

The GP Three Wise Men

Local Medical Councils may have local Three Wise Men committees as well. They were rarely mentioned, however, in these interviews. The implication is that they are not widely used; nor is the BMA Ethics Committee.
LMC chair:

> The GP Three Wise Men, which was the chair of the LMC and two senior members of the LMC, meet on an *ad hoc* basis. The BMA has an Ethical Committee of six well-known consultants and GPs. We could have come to them but they are rarely used. These are the only cases I remember that approach legal jurisdiction.

The royal colleges and their regional advisers

The royal colleges have to approve all training posts for junior doctors. These include vocational training posts for GPs and training posts for junior hospital doctors. Where there are what appear to be insurmountable problems, these posts may be closed by the royal college. It is also possible, but rare, that colleges can threaten removal of one's membership in the royal college. The examples collected all refer to the Royal College of Surgeons. One may assume that the Royal College of General Practitioners can and has withdrawn training posts as well. Royal colleges may also be called upon to evaluate the health of a consultant or give advice on their problems.

> You can use a royal college power position to persuade and coerce. I know about several problem surgeons who were hauled in front of the president of the Royal College of Surgeons who told them to shape up or lose their fellowships in the RCS.
>
> (Consultant surgeon)

> As of January 1990, there is a confidential phoning system. It's integrated with all the royal colleges. It's to identify the 'bad' doctors and protects the identity of the phoner.
>
> (Consultant surgeon)

> The conflict between the two cardiovascular surgeons became so bad that the Royal College of Surgeons took away their training posts.
>
> (Academic hospital manager)

You can always pressure the doctors by a review of their junior doctors' training programmes.

(Regional Director of Public Health)

Some colleagues became concerned about the techniques of a consultant surgeon who had been in place for four years. They came to the RDPH and they went to the Royal College of Surgeons who sent out a vice-president to talk to him. They got him to agree to limit what he was doing; they also talked to his private hospital about the same agreement.

(Regional Director of Public Health)

DISCUSSION

The number of sources of information about potential problems among GPs is remarkable. Yet most of the GP's clinical work is carried out in the privacy of the examining room with no one else around. So information is necessarily tentative until a documented complaint is registered or untoward results are seen by a hospital doctor or on a GP rota. The consultant surgeon cannot work without the assistance of the anaesthesiologist, operating room nurses and junior members of the firm. But the issue of verification remains for both groups of doctors.

Verification is constrained by all the elements of professional etiquette, all the ways in which doctors think about their work that have been discussed in Chapter 2. All these impede belief, assessment and taking any steps. This is underscored repeatedly in the anecdotes and cases throughout this study.

The repertoire of informal mechanisms – the quiet chat, protective support, diverting work – are those one would find in any work setting. They are a reasonable set of approaches to trying to solve workplace problems. And doctors, both consultant surgeons and GPs, attempt to use them. Sometimes they are effective, other times not. The correlates of effectiveness appear to include previous relationships, the nature and severity of the problem, the personality of the problem doctor and the skills of the colleague taking the action.

This study reports more activity than discovered in the American research, certainly more among senior consultants, than Bosk finds in his study of American surgeons.[7] It is likely that the nature of employment in the NHS and the existence of lifelong contracts for hospital consultants can explain the difference. The senior GPs, as independent contractors, have great independence in their work but the FHSAs and the CHCs have formal access to information and complaints, as do the LMCs. These bodies all have responsibilities for the problem GP, although the boundaries between their responsibilities are often not clear to the groups themselves.

Of course, the presence of more mechanisms of regulation and self-regulation does not necessarily produce more effective self-regulation. This is a subject for further investigation and discussion.

Collegial action: corporate responsibility

The hospital Three Wise Men procedure is an unusual quasi-formal mechanism of self-regulation and professional responsibility. It is a recognized system for discrete internal review; it can, ideally, establish facts and recommend next steps. The perception of its effectiveness is highly varied. Some doctors see it as a positive and useful tool, others as a device for cynical manipulation. Some managers have a great deal of respect for its integrity; others see it as just another technique for 'closing ranks'. One can speculate that it can be both and more.

One's role in the health-care delivery system, managerial philosophy and style dictate how one sees the use of the Three Wise Men procedure. The anecdotal evidence is that sometimes it works and sometimes not – and that, in some regions, it is used for more than its original intent, which was to gather factual information about sick doctors. A great deal depends on the skills of the doctors appointed to the committee. Sometimes the Regional Director of Public Health is kept informed and sometimes not; sometimes he can initiate the procedure.

In 1990, the Department of Health suggested the Three Wise Men be expanded to Four Wise Men and that there should always be a psychiatrist and the chair of the Medical Council among them, as well as other senior and respected consultants.[8] This is a useful step. But more important in enhancing the work of this valuable mechanism is formal training for the 'Wise Men' so that they can be consistently skilled as they carry out these difficult tasks.

Pushing a partner out of a GP partnership is a double-edged sword. It rids the partners of a GP they find too suspicious to continue working with. It can protect the reputation of the partnership. It also has the unfortunate effect of 'exporting' the problem. According to the anecdotal material, the partner who is forced out often ends up in single-handed practice. If the problem was one of some form of incompetence, then the GP's behaviour is even more hidden from view and correction even more difficult.

The royal colleges appear to play a positive role in informal ways.

We have already seen that managers may be informed that informal or quasi-formal approaches to problem doctors are in process. They may even assist with them. The cases reveal that when the informal and quasi-formal professional efforts do not produce desired results or break down, managers are brought more directly, if reluctantly, into the case. They have their own repertoire of informal and quasi-formal mechanisms to employ before turning to the formal and drastic measures they can, legally, institute.

4

FRUSTRATION MOUNTS: REQUIRING 'THE SKILL OF A POLITICIAN AND THE TACT OF A DIPLOMAT'

I've used the golden handshake only twice. Once, with the anaesthesiologist who has a drug problem. I told him: 'You're too ill to continue working, because of your back.' If you become satisfied there is no cure but the removal of a doctor, there are two issues: the cost of getting rid of the guy; and a question of confidence in the NHS from the public's point of view. If you have to sack someone two or three times a year, the public will lose confidence. And our responsibility is to do everything to keep our consultants employed.

(Regional Director of Public Health)

In another case of an alcoholic GP, his wife, a trained nurse, ran the practice. His colleagues would go in a real emergency. But many patients in that practice were on inappropriate medications. It's very difficult to have a doctor in that position. Just too dangerous to continue practice. For three years, his colleagues tried to bring pressure on him to retire, with no effect. He became ill, then recovered. His illness was used as an excuse for him to retire. A principal from a neighbouring practice said to him: 'Use the illness to retire or I will spill the beans.' He did retire, it was easier under the cover of illness. It's almost impossible otherwise. It can go on for years unless someone flips overnight. Things tend to come out when something goes horribly wrong. It comes out that people knew but never did anything about it.

(LMC secretary)

MANAGERS GET IN ON THE ACT: AN
IMPORTANT SUPPORTING ROLE

The manager's broad repertoire of mechanisms: the formal and the informal

As the informal approaches break down or fail to resolve the problems, colleagues or the official medical staff representative turn to management for assistance. In settings where various levels of management have good rapport with doctors, they have been aware that informal efforts have been tried; they may even have helped plan them. Where such rapport is weak, managers may not know about a problem or its details, until the informal efforts fail. At this point, the problem has often become complicated and tangled.

Until recent changes, it was the Regional Director of Public Health who was the final responsible manager for hospital problems, since this office managed the consultants' contracts except in teaching districts. Now these are managed at the district or trust hospital level. For GPs, the Family Health Services Authorities are responsible for contracts. The formal powers of the FHSAs are restricted to breaches of contract terms and involve a series of fines. The formal managerial powers in relation to consultant contracts are more elaborate.[1]

Formal disciplinary actions and hospital consultants

While our interest is in the informal approaches that managers attempt when problem doctors are 'turned over' to them, it is important to understand the formal mechanisms managers can call upon. These stand as veiled threats, looming behind the informal mechanisms.

Rooted in employment law, district procedures, General Whitley Council regulations, and government (Department of Health) documents, managers have a small number of disciplinary protocols which are complex and time-consuming. For offensive personal conduct that might include theft, fraud, assault, lateness, absenteeism, abuses to staff, criminal offences outside work and 'bloodymindedness',[2] managers can invoke the district authorities' local disciplinary procedures, Section 40 of the *General Whitley Council Handbook*, or general employment law. For professional misconduct and fitness to practice, the relevant approach is laid out in a Department of Health circular, the most recent version of which is HC (90)9, replacing the long-standing HC (61) 112.[3] Every district and region is required to follow the procedures laid out in this document. This protocol can lead to the suspension and dismissal of a doctor. Only the decision of the appropriate committee of the General Medical Council can lead to suspension of registration or losing registration to practise medicine.

There are also a variety of other formal bars to employment which may affect a hospital consultant. These include certain technical, legal bars to employment such as loss of registration, failure to obtain appropriate qualifications, and refusal to comply with a reorganization.

As will be revealed, the use of any of the formal mechanisms comes with high cost, higher than is generally known. Among other things, the consultants involved will call upon their defence societies or the legal profession for assistance to fight suspension and dismissal. Effective informal approaches to problems are greatly preferred and managers have a broad range of them to call upon, many more than colleagues themselves have created to deal with problem doctors, particularly in the hospitals. The major managerial informal mechanisms are: *depersonalizing criticism*; *re-education* and *job change*; *replanning resources*; and the '*dignity bribe*'.

Depersonalizing the criticism

Managers report, in a small number of cases, quietly arranging for internal or external reviews of problem doctors but in such a way that the doctor is not overtly under criticism or attack. The unit may be reviewed, budgets may be shifted, facilities may be improved, or new positions created as a way to mitigate the problem.

The inside review (other than the Three Wise Men)

The very articulate father of a patient who died complained directly to the head manager who talked to me. I agreed we should call for the case notes. We found the complaint had several features that indicated true incompetence on the part of one consultant and poor management on the part of all the doctors. This was regarding a complex head injury. We asked another very senior consultant for a confidential report. He did that after speaking to the consultants and the junior doctors. He recommended certain actions but no formal procedures.

We set up a working party headed by the chair of the medical staff and including leading doctors who also run an Accident and Emergency unit and involving neurosurgeons to look into the proposals and recommend how they could be implemented. They sat for three months and provided us with a second, public report. This was on how to strengthen the A & E, and out of that came a stream of action. Some of what has been implemented includes a new CT scanner, a computer-based information system and the recommended appointment of a traumatologist.

The doctors involved in the case know they were being investigated. There has been no formal action but they know that the organization is committed to organizational change.

(Health Authority general manager)

The outside review
The outside review, as a managerial mechanism, overlaps with professional resources. It calls upon other consultants inside or outside the region; it calls upon the services of the royal colleges and their regional advisers. It requires co-operation between administration and the profession.

There has been a series of complaints against an orthopaedic surgeon. Four in the last year. Very serious. Failure to diagnose a broken back and left the patient sitting up in a wheelchair. The family complained; the mother is a nurse. Complaints have been going on for several years. I called consultant friends; they wouldn't let their cat near him.

I was seeing the district administrator about him this morning. We've talked several times in the last few months. They don't have the power to do anything. This morning they said a new director of A & E is coming next spring. They are going to do a medical-nursing audit of one of the hospital wards in this service. This will involve the Regional Director of Public Health with the Royal College of Surgery. If I hadn't had a satisfactory answer from the district, I would go to the region.

This consultant may not know there is a case building up against him. These guys have so much independence. He is doing private work too, and there are complaints from private patients. There is not much managerial role in NHS hospitals. Managers are not that professional. Consultants are terrifically independent.

(Community Health Council secretary)

Re-education and job change
The case of an anaesthesiologist comes to mind. Two networks were operating. His peer group, other surgeons and

anaesthesiologists in the same district. The surgeons made me aware that they were unhappy to have their cases in his hands. The other anaesthesiologists said they were aware of this and were looking into the facts. The DDPH told me about it as well. When I got the facts, I went to see him and laid the information before him. He had been practising 15 years, was in his late fifties and had reached a plateau with an old style of practice. Eventually, he agreed to go away for six months for retraining. I used an element of threat, to remove him from his job using HC(61)112 or send the case to the GMC. He accepted retraining and came back to a supervised position. This case ended satisfactorily. I got a report of competence up to a certain level.

(Regional Director of Public Health)

There was a drug-addicted GP who was eventually prosecuted. Like all court cases involving doctors, his was reported to the GMC. He was fined by the courts and lost his job as a GP. In order to help him pay the fine, I gave him a clinical advisory job in my department. The GMC admonished him and put restrictions on his ability to practise. He stayed in the job I created for him for quite a long time and developed considerable expertise in child psychiatry.

His own psychiatrist declared him cured and we made an effort with the GMC to clear him. The GMC restored his prescribing privileges and he got a job as a consultant child psychiatrist. In one year, he had committed suicide – just couldn't take the pressure. We failed to pick up the signals although we made a high effort for years. Yet, another GP we approached in the same way was successful.

(Regional Director of Public Health)

Replanning resources

There was a surgical specialist who came directly to my attention because I was talking to him in the hospital about what he was doing. It was just a normal conversation. I observed directly that he was doing some procedures that fell outside the remit of his post. He had been there many years. There was no question of a patient complaining or another professional saying an outcome wasn't right. He was using resources and staff which were not normally at the disposal of a person carrying out that kind of job. My anxieties were raised directly.

I asked myself: 'Is he competent for these procedures?' I felt I should deal with it and I asked him what he was doing. Then, back in the office, I looked at his job description and CV and became even more anxious. I spoke to one or two senior people who did use those procedures. They were non-committal and I didn't mention any names to them. I then approached the representative of the Royal College of Surgery in our region and asked if he would obtain an RCS review on the matter, still without telling a name.

The RCS actually was unhelpful. The answer was: he's a consultant, he should know what he's doing; if the patients are satisfied . . . I had thought I would be able to go into it further with the regional adviser. This didn't relieve my anxieties about what might happen to patients. I tolerated it for two years. Meanwhile, there was some forward planning in his department. In open discussions, we were able to limit resources to him. I 'planned him out' quite openly. I remember trying to deal with it anonymously. I'm quite prepared to say I was wrong to be stopping him. I might have limited people from getting some help. He didn't know. There was just an atmosphere change.

(Retired Regional Director of Public Health)

In a small general hospital, 25 miles from here, I began to get signals from the hospital manager who is responsible to me that things were not going well in their Accident and Emergency. I felt that some of the problems had to do with a poor physical environment. We designed a new A & E facility, up to modern standards, but the government said there was no money. So I got together a group of business and political leaders in town who raised the money. I felt we cracked one part of the problem. But I was still getting reports from the manager. The nurses said it was hard to get hold of the senior consultant. He wouldn't come and the juniors were just too young. We feel the senior staff were not pulling their weight. It's hard to get hard evidence but the anecdotes are too strong to ignore.

I asked the hospital manager and the District Medical Officer to fill me in on the two consultant surgeons who provide services. I found out about these two. The first has both a managerial and clinical role; the second just clinical. The first has a long number of years at the hospital and is well known as a county personality, very independent, a 'consultant is king' kind. It is substantiated that when the nurses bleep, he's quite unresponsive. The second has made clear that he is not so interested in A & E and this is now showing in his practice. To make matters worse, there have been one or two complaints from patients who were handled badly. For example there was a road accident involving a young boy and a series of possible clinical misjudgements and errors. He is now a paraplegic. It was a complex case but probably poorly supervised.

So I had on my hands a hospital that ten years ago was run by GPs, now becoming an active local district hospital with a poorly performing A & E: the front door of the hospital. I couldn't tie down any performance that would permit me to use formal procedures. Here's what I did.

These two consultants had been complaining for years that they have been running a 1 and 2 rota and were very busy. This is a difficult argument for what they are really doing, but they are right by national norms which are 1 and 3. We didn't respond because a new consultant costs £½ million a year. But we now said we'll appoint a third consultant but only one consultant secretary. They were startled. We also said we will take some general surgery from you two and this new person will be the director of the A & E.

They have now accepted this and we are advertising. It may happen that one will leave. They'll wait and see whom we get. All of this requires the skill of a politician and the tact of a diplomat.

(Health Authority general manager)

I am grateful for reading this [case] because I now feel that I can't let it rest. They [the parents] raise complex but sufficient [evidence]. I now will share this with the chair of the district authority and some of the consultants named in the diary. They will remember the case. Again I feel that some organizational changes are in prospect here. For a long time we've been crazy to offer children's services on eight different sites. There should be a children's centre under the same roof. We may be able to debate this over such a case rather than in the abstract.

(Health Authority general manager)

The 'dignity bribe' (early retirement)

Managers in both the hospital and the GP sectors may try to negotiate early retirement with a problem doctor. One of the FHSA lay chairs described this as a 'dignity bribe'; an RDPH as a 'golden handshake'. To many managers, it is superior to the protracted suspension proceedings.

The lay chair of a London FHSA describes efforts at her previous FHSA to use informal techniques to encourage elderly GPs, in their eighties and nineties, working on their own, to retire.

> We used the nicest sort of blackmail. We'd say: 'Everyone thinks so highly of you. Don't you think you ought to take the initiative now on your own?' The LMC was co-operative in helping, getting peers to make the suggestions. We managed to achieve a number of retirements. I hope we can do the same in this area, although of course there is now mandatory retirement at 70.
>
> The most difficult problems are the alcoholics and the hard-core incompetents. You must take the very tough step and say: 'You must retire.' The hospital consultants are a tea-party compared to the GPs. It is much easier to define good practice in hospitals.
>
> But changes are coming and we are confident that managers will have far more control as managers in hospitals now do. All these problems will be easier for the new FHSAs to deal with.

Here is another account from an LMC secretary:

> Three GPs were involved in a complaint about a man's late wife which culminated in a Medical Services Committee hearing where they were not found in breach of their NHS contract. I knew two of the partners and then met the third. One of them said to me: 'I hope my partner will be OK. He's not well.' It turned out he had Parkinson's and was getting treatment. He was 58 and was forgetful.
>
> I formed the judgement that he should consider retirement but the senior partners found it very difficult to tell him to stop. I encouraged them to talk and they did. 'Why not retire with dignity before you make a mistake?' He came to me and seemed relieved that it was suggested he retire. A lot of doctors don't have any other interests but he is a musician. He's applying for early retirement.
>
> He did have Parkinson's but patients are terribly loyal. And the doctors find it difficult to deal with these things. They're not trained to deal with this and shovel it off on me. I'm objective and fair. I protect the doctor from himself.
>
> Of course, the pension can become an issue. It depends on

how long you have been in the NHS. If you retire on the grounds of ill health, let's say at 54, they would add an additional maximum factor of six years. The less the earnings, the less willingness to take the pension. In most of these cases the GPs are in their fifties, there are no kids at home but it depends on how good the practice has been and their age.

A Regional Director of Public Health had to deal with a consultant near retirement.

He had a coronary and during an emergency operation went into renal failure. After a year, his GP and personal consultant said he could go back to work. But his local colleagues told the RDPH: 'He won't be able to do the work. Get him to retire.' You need 40 years to get your full pension. The man didn't have his 40 years yet and didn't want to retire. His colleagues felt he wasn't pulling his full weight (and hadn't been even before).

I told him: 'You can't go back to work but I'll pay your salary until I can sort it out.' Our occupational health people said he's really OK. I sought another medical opinion through the Royal College of Physicians and got someone else to see him. I told the local colleagues what I was doing and they keep lobbying [for his retirement]. This man saw the outside consultant twice and has been told what will be written to me. I think he will accept early retirement but he's looking for a package where he can have some paying work. I am making enquiries about other work. This is taking a lot of time and phone calls for everyone. He's from a district with a lot of consultant problems. Other districts take care of their own problems.

An academic hospital manager had the problem of a director who was tired and failing to perform.

It was necessary to see how he could be eased out of post. Discussions of an oblique nature started. He was retiring in two, three years. We worked towards early retirement and did it very gradually. The chap in question was likely to receive an 'A' merit award. We wanted him to get that to make it easier to induce retirement. He recently got it. We will press for his retirement. He will exist with a degree of dignity. I have also done a deal so that beds will be preserved [in that unit]. This case took two and a half years to resolve and was probably building up even longer before that.

A Regional Director of Public Health says:

In cases involving doctors within five years or so of retirement (for consultants, this is usually at age 65 to 67) an informal effort will be made to persuade the doctor to retire early. This is most common in cases of impairment or where the problems can be 'medicalized'. Such an effort always involves the Regional Director of Public Health who may call upon others (staff of the British Medical Society or the Protection Society or Defence Union) to help persuade a truculent or recalcitrant doctor. The 'buyout' or 'golden handshake' is increasingly attempted in severe cases as a last resort, in an effort to make early retirement more palatable. This can only be negotiated by the RDPH.

The money for a buyout has to be weighed against loss of confidence in the NHS and the cost of instituting HC (61) 112; this takes people's time and £¼ million.

Stalemate and marginalization

If nothing obtains the desired results, the situation ends in a stalemate. The problem doctor continues in his position and is usually marginalized. Patients have been diverted, resources may be diverted as well. Sometimes the problem doctor can find other sources of patients, may develop research interests or find some other professional way to occupy time until retirement.

A consultant in a diagnostic specialty was making inaccurate reports to the doctor in charge. The volume of complaints about how hopeless his reports were reached a crescendo. They came from many, many sources, both formal and informal. Formally people said: 'You know we are trying to change things in our department.' Informally they said: 'We can't deal with this. What are you going to do about it?' It became common gossip. We had made a terrible mistake. How could we have let him in?

His colleagues talked to him about the quality of his reports. The DDPH talked to him. The chap had no insight. 'I'm doing my best. I've been published. I got a prize.' They stopped referring cases to him and referred cases to departments elsewhere in the region and in the country. This happened during the first year of his appointment. He became very aggressive. 'Why aren't I getting cases?' He complains to the RDPH. All sorts of suggestions are made. More education; only do a limited amount of work. It was like talking to a brick wall.

He gets marginalized, his department shrivels. No one applies for his junior posts. He runs around making work in medical societies; writing; getting published. He seems busy. Gradually, resources that were to be supporting his post get redistributed. We end up with a costly disgruntled person just sitting there, drawing his salary. This goes on for years with various approaches made to shift work, to take early retirement. You're between the devil and the deep blue sea. If you put him to work, he puts patients at risk. So you just carry the cost.

(Regional Director of Public Health)

There was a nationally known psychiatrist with an alcohol problem. He got no support from his peer group. He was allowed to go on until retirement . . . four years. He could have retired early but there was no major accident, no litigation, no major complaints that came to my level.

(District Director of Public Health)

There is a radiologist here who is quite difficult. Maybe there are some errors of judgement but he is a difficult personality. In the past, we were careful to scrutinize reports that came from his department. If something is seriously wrong, you can move. But at the end of the day, 11–164 is really impossible and nasty. It is not a good mechanism. And it is difficult to control the flow of patients if there are a limited number of consultants. You can only control the flow a bit. This radiologist gives good service to GPs. He calls immediately so he gets a lot of work from them but not a lot of work from hospital consultants.

(District Director of Public Health)

There is a neurophysiology consultant, an overseas doctor; probably incompetent. Tests are more painful for patients than they should be; others think this consultant's opinions are not valid. But there may be problems of personal antagonism. I am trying to find another job for him but I've failed so far. For the time being, this consultant's work is limited but remains on full salary.

There was an ENT surgeon . . . perhaps he was incompetent but it couldn't be proven. He got his registrar to do his operations. We instituted an external review and the man assiduously refused to acknowledge any such arrangements. When I arrived [in the job as RDPH] I tried to improve the situation. I looked at his age, just two years until retirement. I adopted what you are calling a marginalization strategy. The leadership of his department was taken away from him and given to another consultant.

(Regional Director of Public Health)

The price of suspension

Some RDPHs have moved to institute the ultimate formal mechanism: suspension and removal from a hospital appointment. The two RDPHs with responsibility for the two regions in this study have conflicting points of view about suspension. The one in the large city sees it as a viable tool, although not one to be used lightly. The RDPH in the less urbanized region made it a point of managerial philosophy never to institute a suspension. Those RDPHs that have used suspension describe it as an unusually difficult and draining experience.

There was a psychiatrist, not directly employed by the region but by a teaching district. His behaviour was becoming irrational and his medical treatments moved from the idiosyncratic to the peculiar, so peculiar as to be questionable whether they were treatments at all. He was already a problem before I came into post. He was known by my predecessor for two years.

The psychiatrist had been suspended by the former area authority and I inherited this. Complaints got more vigorous and moved to the point where his clinical competence was questioned. He became aggressive but resisted suggestions for a vacation, for retraining. The chair [of the region] thought that consultants should be kept in their place and ordered him suspended. The authority dismissed him without an inquiry. He appealed to the Secretary of State who directed the district to hold a proper inquiry. But allegations were hard to prove. I didn't doubt that he should have been suspended but it took a solicitor two years to get evidence.

The big catch was that many of the witnesses refused to testify. It came to an inquiry which recommended dismissal. He appealed, which took two years. The Secretary of State pointed out that it took seven years to do all this. He wanted alternative employment but no one would take him. The Secretary of State confirmed his dismissal. The psychiatrist went to civil court and got nowhere.

The basic problem is that the chap was an [overseas] doctor.

Their cultural set is that consultants are demigods so they won't take advice and instruction except from someone who is their superior. I tried to get him to go to a special course in London. He would say: 'There is nothing I need to learn.' He was offered holiday. He denied any need with hostility and rudeness. Other consultants tried to talk to him, medical officers, administrators. There were seven years of suspension before he was dismissed. He got a salary and he was a full-time locum. That was £550,000, and other expenses totalled £1,000,000. That case was a national record.

There is also the case of the consultant suspended six or seven years ago on full pay. This is not resolved but it is not as costly as going through the firing process which would cost tens of thousands of pounds.

(Retired Regional Director of Public Health)

This region has never had a suspension. It is almost a matter of principle. The most difficult case is someone who has become incompetent. This is where 61–112 is applicable but we have never used it. These cases are always solved informally.

(Retired Regional Director of Public Health)

I had an awful experience. The case is in court now and it has altered my style. The Three Wise Men couldn't exclude the possibility that a doctor was ill and he refused to have a medical exam. So I had to start a 61–112 procedure. In the enquiry, it came out that there was a conspiracy against this doctor in the hospital. He was involved in a custody battle over children in a divorce case. He took us to court and he won. He took his colleagues to court for libel and settled out of court. After 61–112 found in his favour and that he had been wronged, he didn't come to work. We terminated him. He went to court and won reinstatement. The NHS is a remarkably closed system. Once you run afoul of the system all the problems are usually personality disorders. The telephones buzz. Getting another job can be impossible.

(Regional Director of Public Health)

Fifteen years ago, a doctor was threatened with suspension. He fought the case and won. He has been a problem ever since.

(Academic hospital manager)

A consultant geriatrician has recently been sacked in this health authority. My understanding is that it is someone who has been known and talked about for years. The problem is a mixture of everything: mild clinical incompetence, slight sexual harassment, a feeling of general discomfort about the man. These are Three Wise Men and Medical Committee type things and were investigated but nobody was ever prepared to give testimony. Then two medical colleagues did agree to give testimony and that started a full-blown investigation. The general manager of his unit suspended and then fired him through HC (62) 114. It has been in appeal for 18 months. Everybody has found the procedure extremely cumbersome and there is strong feeling that he can't come back to work.

(Academic hospital manager)

The suspension of doctors in the NHS has occasionally become a public issue. One of the most famous cases of suspension in the NHS was that of consultant obstetrician Wendy Savage at the London Hospital Medical College.[4] Challenged by the seniors in her department as incompetent, a long and well-publicized battle vindicated Dr Savage. The original motives for suspension appeared to have been a serious and long-term personality conflict complicated by sharply differing clinical philosophies. The institution of this suspension cost the NHS millions of pounds and months of adverse publicity in the national press. It is an example of the intertwining and confounding factors that lie behind discussions of alleged incompetence. And it is a striking example of the price paid for using the formal mechanisms to deal with problems.

In 1988 the government produced a report on revising hospital suspension proceedings[5] which was followed by a report of a professional working party.[6] While neither report was able to produce reliable time-series data, the latter suggests that '1 in 50 senior hospital doctors will experience [suspension] sometime in their professional lifetime'.[7] Both reports comment on how costly the procedure is, in terms of both money and emotional trauma, for all involved. But each report stresses different aspects of the issue, one the managerial and the other the professional. The suspension procedures were streamlined after these reports, but the problems remain. One set of statistics produced by the professional report indicates that at the time of their study, the Trent and Metropolitan regions used suspension 200 and 300 per cent more than regions like Oxford, South West and Wessex. And, according to the report, doctors born outside the UK, female doctors, doctors in metropolitan regions, paediatricians and psychiatrists are at highest risk of suspension.[8]

THE SPECIAL PROBLEMS OF THE IMPAIRED DOCTOR

As mentioned before, in a significant number of the cases described, impairment – alcoholism, mental and physical illness, drug addiction, senility – is suspected or is one of the problems.

> You know the definition of an alcoholic, don't you? Someone who drinks more than his doctor. Can an alcoholic be a good doctor? . . . It amazes me, the way patients put up with things. The old style ethic. Patients will live with many things. A doctor had been complained about, fined. You go to his list one year later and 50 per cent of those complainants are still there. Patients don't stop their doctors very readily.
>
> A single-handed practitioner gave terrific service for 25–30 years. He drank heavily for at least 20 years, showed all the signs of being an alcoholic for ten years, also signs of drug dependence. In World War II, under difficulty, he ran services for the community doing heroic things. This was a remote rural area. He did surgeries in different places. He stops for a whisky at the top of a particular hill. Patients would catch him, with their big problems, at the top of the hill (before he took his drink). Sometimes patients think it reflects on them. Is something lacking in them if the doctor has taken to the bottle?
>
> (Former Department of Health RMO)

> A lady doctor, eastern European in background, set up a horrendous surgery, bad premises. She didn't drive a car so she walked or rode a bike to visit patients. There were complaints from nurses, social workers, other doctors. She was out of date in her knowledge. She didn't understand paperwork. Probably, she had started out as a good doctor.
>
> We were, at one stage, guardian angels, trying to help. She had a fall and went to rehabilitation. We tried to persuade her to retire but she ignored us. In the end, she did retire. She may have been mentally unstable. We couldn't get her to apply for her pension. For two years she didn't reply to anything, including the GMC. She was taken off the Register so she had to stop practising.
>
> (LMC secretary)

> A friend had a partner who was charming when sober and incompetent when drinking. The partner noticed and tried to

get him into treatment. It didn't work. They went to the Defence Society and asked for remedies. They went through the partnership agreement but got no practical help. Just wait until the problem gets worse or get him to retire. My friend was stuck with this doctor, who was in his forties.

The problem ended abruptly. My friend heard noises from this doctor's room. The doctor was drunk and set himself on fire with a cigarette. He resigned from the group and didn't appear in that patch again.

(LMC chair)

A case was reported to the GP Three Wise Men. We investigated one where the GP was thought to be acting peculiarly. There was suspicion of mental impairment. What we found was a bit of obsessive behaviour but difficulty in saying if it was more than eccentricity.

(Senior GP)

How long would a partnership carry a sick doctor? It depends on the extent to which it affects their work. There is the case of the surgeon who became an alcoholic. He accepted treatment and decided he wanted to be a GP. We took him in. He lapsed once or twice. It didn't affect the patients; he just wouldn't come to the office. We tolerated it. But he relapsed sufficiently so that he resigned himself. We parted best of friends.

(LMC Chair)

The second case was kept from common knowledge. This is a case where the GP was on barbiturates. The patients noticed that she wasn't right in clinic and a partner contacted me. I went [to see her] and challenged her: 'What are you on?' Her husband went with me and we found drugs in her purse. The next step was that she suspended herself from duty. We got a psychiatrist to see her and take her on. She came back to practise and lapsed again. Then she left the district and went elsewhere as a locum. She was picked up by the police for odd behaviour and I was contacted to keep her out of the courts. She was brought to the GMC and lost her right to prescribe. Then we got her a job doing pathology in a district hospital. Now, we have lost touch. All this happened over a year's period.

(LMC chair)

A GP was thought to be handing out tablets too freely. He had rented space in a health centre and the social worker noticed a fair run of undesirable people. She contacted the manager who contacted the LMC. It was looked into and discovered that he was taking them, too. He was sent away for six months of treatment. It was possibly a year before we got to him. Some families threatened to sue but that was never done.

(Senior GP)

What these stories reveal

In general, there are three aspects to each of these cases: the process of identifying the problem; the response of the problem doctor; and the nature of the outcomes.

The process

It takes considerable time to recognize and properly identify most forms of impairment, which often develop gradually. For example, it is difficult to distinguish alcoholism from acceptable norms of social drinking; it can be difficult to distinguish the line between impairment and 'eccentric' behaviour. There is reticence to confront a colleague. Patients may have strong loyalty to the impaired doctor after years of good service.

The response of the problem doctor

It may be hard to accept a diagnosis. There is often an unwillingness to accept treatment. If treatment is accepted, there may be recidivism. There is an unwillingness to accept retirement.

Outcomes

The cases reflect a variety of outcomes: treatment and success; treatment–recidivism–treatment; retirement; refusal and isolation; job change. One type of job change that appears several times is that to locum. This poses a dilemma. It is reasonable that a trained doctor, under treatment for an illness but able to work, should have the opportunity to do so. Indeed, it may be important for self-esteem as well as treatment; it may be important for financial reasons. Yet it appears that it is difficult to predict when this may put patients at risk.

There has been an increased interest in the impaired doctor in the last ten years and efforts have been made to approach problems in more reasonable and helpful ways. There is also a growing research literature which provides systematic information.

Research on the impaired doctor

Doctors are at excessive risk for some physical illnesses. For example, they have a three times higher rate of cirrhosis of the liver than the general population.[9] Indeed, while the standard mortality ratio for lung cancer in doctors has fallen far more steeply than that for the general population over a period of 40 years, that for liver cirrhosis in doctors has risen at an inverse rate. Doctors are also twice as likely to die in road accidents as the general population;[10] and have a higher rate of accidental poisoning.[11] Psychiatric illness presents the biggest threat to doctors, with rates of suicide, affective psychosis and alcohol and drug dependency exceeding those in the general population.[12] Doctors have a three times higher suicide rate than the population at large.[13]

A 1991 study of addicted doctors in treatment reports on a population of 141 addicted doctors from one treatment programme's records.[14] The author's study of these 141 cases provides systematic information about such doctors. The average age when treatment was sought was 43.1 and it took over 6 years from the time when complications started until referral took place. In the interim, the doctors 'suffered increasing physical, psychological and social damage'.[15] Forty-two per cent of the cases involved GPs and 40.2 per cent hospital doctors. The two specialties at greatest risk were anaesthesiologists and GPs. The latter were usually single-handed, as their illness led to practice break-up. Substance abuse began when the doctors were in their twenties and thirties.

When the problem becomes overwhelming, circumstances force treatment, 58 per cent through medical referral and 28.5 per cent because of defence society and GMC involvement.[16] Because of the embarrassment in confronting an addicted colleague and the uncertainty about the usefulness of treatment, years pass, nothing is done and a valuable professional is wasted.

The causes of doctors' high rates of psychiatric illness are thought to include stress, anxiety and depression, and easy access to and knowledge of drugs. It has been suggested that medical associations do not act as supportive groups, and that they leave their members to deal alone with ever increasing demands, possibly predisposing them to depression and suicide. The medical career structure is also seen as an important source of stress – the job insecurity, frequent need to move, prolonged training and long hours.[17]

It has also been noted that doctors do not readily present themselves as unwell to their colleagues. Richards, in his study of GPs as patients, discovered that doctors will readily present 'medical' problems such as a suspicious lump to a colleague for advice. But they are much more reluctant to present illnesses that have implications of weakness or being unable to cope, such as headache, insomnia, sexual problems, or alcohol or drug dependence. These are the very illnesses to which doctors are the most vulnerable.[18]

Efforts to help: National Counselling Service

In October 1985 the royal colleges and faculties, the Joint Consultants Committee and the BMA, set up a National Counselling and Welfare Service for sick doctors. The National Counselling Service, though it receives financial support from the Department of Health, is an autonomous, confidential service. Doctors cannot be referred directly from it to the GMC. The service is controlled by a National Management Committee. It has appointed a number of national advisers who are senior doctors representing all disciplines (including a large number of psychiatrists). After an informal contact by the doctor in need or a colleague (via a national contact telephone number), the national adviser or a nominated specialist will contact the sick doctor. They make an offer of help appropriate to his or her needs, and outside the district in which he works. No records are kept at any central point. This essential confidentiality will, it is hoped, enable doctors to take up various offers of help. (About a quarter of the calls received come from the sick doctors themselves.[19])

It has been noted that a disadvantage of this service is that probably only a small proportion of the sick doctors in Britain are put into contact with the programme. Those running the service have recognized that its 'true effectiveness as a preventive and therapeutic agent remains unknown because of the strict secrecy surrounding its operations'.[20]

Efforts to help: General Medical Council Health Committee

The GMC's central machinery for dealing with a sick doctor acts in response to a report from somebody anxious about a doctor's health

– for example, a Local Medical Committee, a member of the public or another doctor. Between August 1980 when the system began, and October 1988, the council received reports on 383 doctors (86 per cent of cases investigated so far have been men). Calls from doctors worried about colleagues may be diverted to the National Counselling Service if it seems that the GMC cannot help because the doctor's fitness to practice is not seriously impaired. Roughly a third of the doctors entering the GMC's health procedure are not examined, another third are successfully rehabilitated, and the remainder are suspended, accept voluntary erasure, or die.[21]

The GMC would like to develop mechanisms for the rehabilitation of sick doctors. They have had a series of meetings with Regional Directors of Public Health attempting to establish sheltered posts for sick doctors returning to practice. These posts might also be used for doctors being rehabilitated after passing through the disciplinary process.

The report on *Doctors Requiring Rehabilitation Following Ill Health* appeared in 1989, the result of these meetings between the GMC and the Regional Directors of Public Health. This reviews the problems of the impaired doctor and possibilities, criteria and protocols for retraining.[22] It also makes a number of recommendations for financing and organization of such a programme. There is no research that reveals how extensive such retraining programmes are for impaired doctors.

The chair of the Health Committee in 1989, while generally pleased with the way the health procedures work, expresses four particular worries. The first of these is that doctors who appear before the committee are often financially impoverished, and that impoverishment may be one reason why some doctors are not represented by their defence societies. Secondly, the relationship between the sick doctor and the medical supervisor appointed by the GMC may be complicated, as the loyalty of the supervising doctor may be divided.

A third defect of the system may be that the GMC has no power over sick medical students, despite evidence that sick doctors' problems commonly begin when they are students.[23] Finally, the success of the system is (partly) dependent upon a report to the relevant authority and there is reluctance on the part of colleagues to make such a report.[24]

The chair of the GMC Health Committee points out that the GMC is only dealing with a small fraction of the sick doctors in Britain, and he is doubtful whether the local machinery is coping adequately. It has been suggested that a tenth of doctors are impaired;[25] this is approximately 10,000 doctors. The GMC has dealt with about 400 doctors in ten years.[26]

The profession's organizational efforts through the national counselling service and the GMC Health Committee are significant improvements over previous patterns of dealing with impaired doctors through the disciplinary machinery. And more work remains to be done. As the Brooke article argues: 'To allow the stricken doctor to continue without intervention denies our duty to colleagues, to patients and to society'.[27]

DISCUSSION

When colleagues cannot or will not take steps, managers must take over the problem. They have their own repertoire of informal mechanisms, a larger one than the doctors have. But in order to use them, there must be acquiescence of the medical leaders, and their co-operation. While the mechanisms are purely managerial, they can be carried out only at the insistence of or co-operation with doctor colleagues. Managers now become agents of doctors in trying to resolve what colleagues have found to be an intractable problem, beyond the capacity of their approaches and their patience.

How soon the manager is made knowledgeable about the problem, the manager's personal rapport with the doctors involved, and the manager's professional skills and managerial philosophy all play a part in effectiveness. The more empathetic the managers are to the profession, the more likely they will be to use informal approaches effectively. The more distant the manager, the more likely will be the use of more formal approaches, with all their costs in time, money and human relationships.

The impaired doctor remains a particular challenge. But more and better research provides insights and increasingly effective tools for detection and treatment.

The use of any of the mechanisms is rife with constraints and questions. What is the nature of the problem? How serious is it in terms of competence? What is the appropriate action? Does the problem persist? What are the appropriate next steps and what will they cost? How skilled and knowledgeable are those who try to deal with the problem? As one manager put it: 'Problem doctors require the skill of a politician and the tact of a diplomat'.

Using the words of those intimately involved in finding out about problem doctors, in finding ways to assess the information that accumulates, and in attempting to do something of an informal nature, we have heard a vivid and varied drama. The question now is how effective these informal mechanisms are, particularly the ones attempted by professional colleagues, one's fellow doctors.

BEHIND CLOSED DOORS: HOW EFFECTIVE ARE THE INFORMAL MECHANISMS?

There is the underlying fear that to report a problem to me is likely to lead to the end of a career rather than to rehabilitation. I had a unanimous vote by a division in one district that this doctor should not come back to work after his second bout of alcoholism and attempted suicide. I got two good reports from outside psychiatrists. I said: 'He is coming back.' I talked to the staff; they thought it was going to be their responsibility to supervise him. I allayed their fears about his coming back, I got medical reports from his psychiatrist; he agreed to this as a condition of his coming back. The recidivism rate is high although it's hard to keep track because some of these people just disappear. There is a 50 per cent relapse rate on alcohol. But I have had some great successes so I keep persuading colleagues to take these doctors back.

(Regional Director of Public Health)

There has been a series of complaints against an orthopaedic surgeon. Four in the last year, very serious. Failure to diagnose a broken back (left the patient sitting up in a wheelchair). The family complained; the mother is a nurse. Complaints have been going on for several years. I called consultant friends; they wouldn't let their cat near him. I was seeing the district administrator about him this morning. We've talked several times in the last few months. They don't have the power to do anything.

(CHC secretary)

Why should a consultant accept early retirement, even with incentives? It's tantamount to admitting something's wrong.

(Academic consultant surgeon)

My rule of thumb is: there is always one [problem] in every district at any one time. You get rid of one; another pops up. Perhaps there are between

16 and 20 in a region – 3–5 per cent of all doctors. I can always see another one coming along. That's the tip of the iceberg.

(Regional Director of Public Health)

What is 'incompetence'? In the cases described, when asked to speak about colleagues who might be incompetent, those interviewed for this study suggest definitions of what they view as incompetence. Judging from these cases, it is an uncertain term that could include lack of knowledge and/or skill; various forms of impairment; temporary personal problems or burnout; and personality conflicts. All of these are perceived to imply defects of knowledge and/or skill. These are clearly differentiated, in the words of those interviewed, from the 'unavoidable' defects of knowledge and skill that doctors see as part of the permanent uncertainty and necessary fallibility of everyday medical practice.

How many 'incompetent' doctors are there in the system at any particular time? No hard data are available. Everyone interviewed felt intuitively that it was a tiny minority among hospital consultant surgeons, particularly because of the long and arduous path to consultancy. Among GPs the estimations were similar. Each appropriate interviewee was asked to estimate the number in his/her hospital, district or region.

These estimates consistently ranged between 3 per cent and 5 per cent. Without clear definitions and further systematic research, it is difficult to assess the accuracy of such estimates.

We have seen that the way in which doctors think about mistakes and accidents in practice makes it difficult for them to identify and judge colleagues' clinical work. But when suspicions are aroused, what do colleagues do, of an informal nature, to carry out their societal obligation to regulate themselves?

WHAT COLLEAGUES DO: PATTERNS AND DETERMINANTS

We have seen that there is a small repertoire of informal mechanisms that the doctors interviewed describe in reported cases: *the quiet chat, protective support, work shifting, being pushed out of the partnership* and *the Three Wise Men procedure*. These are all, however, constrained by several important patterns of behaviour. Among those patterns are the following:

Delaying action as long as possible

There is a persistent unwillingness to act, to 'grasp the nettle' as several interviewees put it. At every stage, as colleagues move from simple to more complex mechanisms, it is difficult to take the necessary steps, from gathering facts and information, through talking to the problem doctor, to instituting measures. An enveloping inertia overcomes those with responsibility.

Protective support is used with considerable selectivity

Protective support, one of the more complex and productive of the informal mechanisms, is only offered to a small number of doctors. It usually involves a doctor who has been respected by colleagues or has had an unusual career. It is usually found where the problem is a product of selected illness such as alcoholism and physical illness. This mechanism engenders group solidarity and a heightened sense of loyalty. It can include junior and senior doctors and nurses; it may even improve the quality of the group's work. It begins to break down when the team feels it is having to work too hard, or the behaviour of the problem doctor becomes too extreme, threatening or overbearing.

Medicalization of the problem makes it easier to deal with

If the problem doctor's problem can be medicalized, it is somewhat easier to deal with if it is a product of being physically 'sick'. Mental illness, the difficult personality, and plain incompetence are harder to accept and harder to deal with. At the same time, it is difficult to be certain of the signs of encroaching illness when one sees someone on a daily basis, as in the hospital; it is equally difficult for doctors to accept that they may be ill themselves, particularly with something that is not a physical illness.

The less it is a recognizable medical problem, the more ambiguous the problem, the less likely the informal mechanisms will be used, and, if they are used, the less likely they will be effective.

As the informal mechanisms break down, the case invariably becomes more complex

The informal mechanisms phase into the quasi-formal (for example, the Three Wise Men) and, if these fail, administrators or managers are drawn into the action. Depending on managerial style, rapport with medical staff and the degree of trust that has built between them, hospital, district or regional managers may know about a case in its early stages. Some RDPHs and hospital unit managers are not aware of a Three Wise Men procedure having been instituted; others are alerted when the first quiet chat takes place. By the time a manager is typically drawn into a case formally, it has already become complex. Attitudes and positions have hardened and are more difficult to deal with. Bringing in a manager is often an admission that the informal professional approaches have not worked.

DETERMINANTS

What are some of the factors that produce patterns like these?

The norms of professional etiquette and equality among peers make it difficult to pass judgement on a fellow doctor. There is also a personal reticence to criticize that grows out of the way doctors think about mistakes. Uncertainty, necessary fallibility and shared vulnerability buttress this reticence. Clinical freedom, particularly among senior doctors, is deeply cherished. All these, along with hesitation to interfere in another's livelihood, combine to delay taking action at all points along the continuum of informal mechanisms.

The quality of interpersonal relations determines the kind of approach taken and certainly whether a problem colleague gets protective support. The nature and degree of collegiality and tolerance for deviance in the group, the problem doctor's previous reputation, the nature of the aberrant behaviour and the quality of previous relations are important factors in whether a problem is identified, how a doctor is approached and how the doctor is dealt with.

The quality of interpersonal and management skills of the colleagues taking responsibility for initiative is important in their success. This is particularly true given the reality of life contracts for consultants in British hospitals and the independent nature of the British GP. There is usually no special training for this role. While the profession says 'Only we can judge each other' and promises self-regulation, it has no particular expertise to do so. Where some individuals in positions of responsibility (an LMC secretary; a RDPH) seem considerably more successful than their colleagues in dealing with problem doctors, their interpersonal and management skill levels are higher.

The nature of doctors' contracts complicates these issues. The life contract given to consultants becomes a factor, as well as the control the profession has exercised over their numbers. While GP partners can terminate a partnership, general practitioner contracts with the FHSAs may be quite easy to obtain in underserved areas. Consultants will be among the best-paid professionals in the NHS. There is no financial incentive for early retirement and certainly no status incentive. The change in upper age limit for general practitioners to 65 will resolve some of the problems described in the GP cases. There is contradictory opinion about the suitability of early pensions, and perceptions differ about how enticing they can be made. In the hospitals, the golden handshake is a growing trend but only because doctors threatened with suspension or actually suspended are increasingly more likely to fight such action.

Comparing consultants and general practitioners

While the thinking about the uncertainties of medical practice is generally similar among the consultants and the GPs in this study, there are some important differences.

The first set of differences concerns *observability* and the *nature of the specialty*. The GP's work is carried out in more private settings than the surgeon's, which necessarily includes junior doctors and operating room nurses. While GP colleagues may pick up clues from a rota, from patient comments, indications of overadmission to hospital, remarks from the CHC secretary, these will be highly fragmented.

Among GPs, it is more the 'suspicious' characteristic that may attract attention, whether or not it is specifically identified with a mistake or accident. While something similar goes on among consultants, there is another element of their work that is taken into consideration: its processes and outcomes are more clear-cut.

While uncertainty, necessary fallibility, shared personal vulnerability, recognition of the egregious error, norms of non-criticism and the strong sentiment that only the profession can make judgements about mistakes are expressed in the interviews with consultant surgeons, there is clearer recognition of avoidable mistakes. This is based on systematic, comparative studies to which some of the surgeons referred.

A consultant surgeon at an academic centre says:

Boundaries [between the avoidable and unavoidable] are drawn by audit and statistical information. A 25 per cent infection rate in hernia operations is not good. Well-recognized patterns are becoming more recognized. If one unit has more infections than another, we need to identify the facts and analyse the cause. It may be the population you are working with . . . there will always be variations . . . it's fearfully difficult to identify small variations. They aren't that important. The big ones are important. Audit should be part of ordinary practice; that's why it is in the White Paper.

And a supervising director of surgery:

You need statistical or corroborative evidence. In my specialty, there never should be damage to [a particular organ]. I do a hundred operations a year and get a 1 per cent damage rate – one or two a year. There is always a percentage who suffer this injury.

Another consultant surgeon notes:

Will these problems arise more often in some than in others? In my field, everybody has a leak incidence but it varies. A middle range of leaks is the norm. Twenty-five to 35 per cent leaks is an unreasonable level. Eighty-five per cent of surgeons, according to a study, knew about this. Feedback of such information can influence future results.

Considerable comparative statistical work has been done in surgery to compare outcomes around Britain. A consultant surgeon knowledgeable about the Confidential Enquiry into Postoperative Deaths (CEPOD) asserts:

You can tell a great deal about individual surgeons by looking at distribution curves. You feed the knowledge to them and they will improve. CEPOD is trying to pick the lowest 20 per cent of surgeons (concerning leak and infection rates) in [Britain]. They range from 3 to 30 per cent. Those with 30 per cent rates changed and improved. Statistical information can make a difference.

The extent to which the individual surgeon pays attention to such peer comparisons and their own ranking in them is a private matter. But these are more precise performance data than yet found in the growing audit efforts for GPs. The nature of the surgical specialties makes this more possible. Even this kind of information cannot overcome the strong sense of autonomy of the consultant surgeon, professional etiquette, and the life contract.

Negotiating a reputation: mistakes, incompetence and how your colleagues regard you

The medical views described above suggest that there is no necessary relationship between making mistakes and incompetence. All doctors make mistakes and accept them as part of normal medical practice. It is only when something extreme occurs, the egregious mistake, and particularly if it happens more than once, and where a doctor does not appear to learn from his mistakes, that suspicions of incompetence arise in the minds of colleagues.

Suspicions are easier to harbour if the doctor is an 'outsider' for some reason or has some suspected impairment or other characteristics. In a world that does not recognize mistakes as the lay world would, which looks at mistakes in a special way, the informal mechanisms of self-regulation are themselves techniques for defining incompetence.[1] Particularly in general practice, doctors can never really define mistakes except for the extreme instance, and even here mitigating circumstances are usually discovered. Mistakes cannot be precisely defined so there is an ongoing negotiation of reputations where the important clues are personal characteristics as often as clinical decisions.

It is when one of the informal, quasi-formal and indeed formal mechanisms is instituted that the boundary between the acceptable and the unacceptable mistakes or behaviour has been identified. This signals the identification of a doctor who is thought to be incompetent by his colleagues. In the 1990s, however, there are stronger pressures than ever to shrink the boundaries of uncertainty, and to define more clearly what is avoidable and what is unavoidable as far as clinical mishaps are concerned.

Are collegial informal mechanisms effective?

Of the cases collected concerning hospital consultant surgeons in the British NHS who were perceived by their colleagues as being incompetent for a variety of reasons, those interviewed expressed dissatisfaction with the management and resolution of somewhat more than half the cases. As for the GPs, leaving aside the problem of the elderly doctor, three-quarters of the cases described end unsatisfactorily. A skilled LMC secretary can be effective, as can a persuasive colleague, but the examples of these are in the minority.

In the majority of the cases, managers have to be brought into an escalating and increasingly complex problem.

MANAGERS: THE IMPORTANCE OF SKILL AND INTERPERSONAL RELATIONS

Working with consultants: the regional directors of public health

The regional director of public health is one of the key administrative managers in the regional health authorities. Until 1991, the hospital consultant contracts were held at regional level. Among other duties, the RDPHs had a major advisory role in the administration of these contracts, except for districts which have teaching hospitals where the consultant contracts were administered by the District Medical Officer. All of the RDPHs are medically trained, usually as community doctors. Many have additional degrees as well. While all consultant contracts are now held at the district level and, in the case of hospitals that have become self-governing trusts, at the hospital level, the previous experience of the RDPHs is of great importance in understanding the use of informal mechanisms in dealing with very troublesome or incompetent doctors.

The experience of the RDPHs has great relevance to the important observation that managerial style – whether it is formal or informal – has a significant impact on how effectively these matters are carried out. The recent changes in the NHS will inevitably bring in new managers who will have to establish themselves and develop new networks of information and collegial relationships. In such a context, there is more reliance on the formal sources of information and formal approaches. As shall be seen, these are often less effective and more costly in terms of time, resources and interpersonal relations.

The repertoire of informal mechanisms used and the extent to which they are used is related to the managerial style developed by a particular RDPH and the characteristics of a particular region. One of the study regions, with a single, internationally known medical school, has had a firm principle of never using suspension. Another region dominated by a large, complex and heterogeneous metropolitan area finds it much more difficult to establish rapport with all its consultants, has instituted suspensions and seems to have a limited repertoire of informal techniques that it is able to use with problem doctors.

**Working with consultants: new hospital unit managers
with old problems**

Two of the managers interviewed are relatively new hospital unit
managers in major academic medical centres. One has a background in the business world; the other has an extensive clinical
background. These two managers reveal important aspects of the
relationship between top hospital managers in the NHS and the
senior doctors, the consultants, around the issue of the problem
doctor.

Building trust

The two managers face the same problem: how to get into
information networks about problem doctors, and a broad range of
other information. One enters the job with considerable insight into
clinical work and the behaviour of the medical profession. As a
former specialty director, this manager has broad experience with
doctors and considerable sympathy but has never been approached
informally concerning a problem doctor. The other, from the world
of commerce, has no comparable experience, although his general
experience in organizations alerts him to the human pressures that
can complicate work and produce incompetence. It takes him two
years of building rapport and trust to reach a point where the
consultants begin to confide in him.

Out of the information networks

The more important point is that these managers are relatively
unaware of the problem doctor and removed from the workings of
the informal mechanisms. This is both appropriate and frustrating.
Both administrators express considerable trust that the informal
mechanisms are working, that the Three Wise Men are 'the most
respected in the district' and that the doctors are dealing with
problems related to incompetence. Both have confidence that the
doctors are taking on medical audit, that audit will be effective and
that, among others, it will help with the incompetence issue. There
is also confidence expressed that as consultants themselves take on
management roles, they will be forced to address incompetence
issues more directly. These are, however, perceptions based on
admittedly little hard information.

A stronger management

Yet both look forward to the changes that will strengthen their hand as managers: the new purchasing contracts, the new consultant contracts and the possibilities that are beginning to emerge (only dimly perceived) in the workings of Crown Indemnity. They would like very much to know more about negligence problems. One manager has been tracking them, at least partially, through the claims that come to the hospital. But both expect to know and do more as the latest reforms in the NHS push along the transformation of their role from administrator to manager.

Working with general practitioners: a national view

Two well-informed Department of Health officials close to the GP complaints procedures discuss their views on the FHSAs, the LMCs, medical audit and the changes coming in the 1990s.

The Family Health Services Authority complaint procedures are based on two principles: the importance of peer review and the focus on breach of contract, not clinical competence which is considered a matter for the courts. When a Family Health Services Authority–Medical Services Committee hears a case against a GP, the emphasis is on whether the doctor has violated the terms of his contract with the NHS. So, for example, if a GP goes on a home visit, examines the patient in a reasonable way and gives the wrong diagnosis, this is not a breach of contract even if he continually misdiagnoses. This is often hard for the consumer to understand as are the detailed procedures that the Family Health Services Authority–MSC requires.

The LMCs are local trade unions for the GPs and looking after their interests. They should be talking to the incompetent doctors but they only do that idiosyncratically. The onus is on them to be dealing with the impaired doctor as well. After all, GPs can still get paid while they are in treatment. There is also concern and criticism of the peer group (the partnership) that pushes out the weakest member into single-handed (and unsupervised) practice.

As for incompetence, that is a very delicate question and one must chose one's words very carefully. We know, and the LMCs know, who the incompetent doctors are. We got quite a lot of information through the Department of Health RDPHs who were advised to talk to the LMCs. But what have the LMCs actually done? Of course, we are talking about a small percentage of GPs – under 5 per cent.

We are confident that the new FHSAs . . . will bring improvements. The new contracts will mandate audit and all the GPs will have to participate. Although it is an early stage of audit, we are hopeful. Also, there will be lower GP representation on the FHSAs (and less domination).

The government has been discussing medical audit with the profession and feels that the profession as a whole has accepted audit. The government now wants the production of outcome measures and has been trying to get the profession interested in this. The Secretary of State has invited all the presidents of the royal colleges to talk about clinical standards.

How effective are managers with informal approaches?

Judging from the case material in this study, a skilled manager who has a rapport with the medical staff is more adept in dealing with these problems than professional colleagues alone. The cases that were most effectively handled were those reported by the RDPHs and LMC secretaries who both understand and are sympathetic to the exigencies of clinical practice, have good interpersonal skills and are also skilled at (and professional about) managing human personnel problems. They are the most inventive, least confrontational and most flexible.

Where they work effectively as a team with doctors, they also support and aid the efforts of colleagues to deal with these problems themselves, and behind closed doors.

Where this can be done, where colleagues can work the problems out themselves or with the assistance of sympathetic managers, there is less acrimony and less time and resources wasted. Of course, managers' collaboration with doctors can also backfire, if the colleagues are 'using' the managers for personal rather than clearly professional and competence reasons. Managers can also antagonize, misidentify, and mishandle problem doctors.

Managers at all levels, working both with GPs and hospital consultants, express the opinion that recent changes in the NHS will improve their and the profession's ability to deal more effectively with problem doctors and incompetence. We will examine this perception more closely in Chapter 7.

COMPARISON WITH RESEARCH IN THE USA AND SWEDEN

Was Shaw accurate in his 1902 characterization of the medical profession, that 'no doctor dare accuse another of malpractice'? Such reticence is clearly documented. 'There is a conspiracy to hide its own shortcomings.' Perhaps some would see protective support as a 'conspiracy'. The profession is still motivated to be protective of its image and to deal with its own problems as long as the problem colleague has not been too deviant and too eccentric. The British medical profession has, however, recently accepted the principles of medical audit and peer review, as long as they are private and remain in the profession's hands.

The playwright had extraordinary insight but did not offer enough explanation. We must turn to the social scientists for systematic analysis, in this case the work done by the Americans Eliot Freidson and Charles Bosk.

Freidson's findings from his study of informal self-regulation among a group of doctors in a health maintenance organization may be summarized as follows:[2]

1 Collegial etiquette forbids criticism of each other.
2 Non-medical opinions of colleagues were devalued.
3 The few informal mechanisms that did exist included:
   (a) withdrawing favours;
   (b) talking to a colleague in an educational manner;
   (c) any real confrontation was by a collective representative, for example the executive committee;
   (d) turning particularly difficult cases over to a reluctant administration.

There are a number of parallel findings in the present study and Freidson's. These are listed in Table 5.1.

More corporate efforts in Britain

Clearly there are similarities in the two countries, although the setting for Freidson's study differs significantly from either the hospital firms of the consultants or the various practice forms of the GPs. It is not reasonable to make close comparisons, but it appears that there are more informal mechanisms and they have more of a corporate nature in Britain. In particular, the Three Wise Men procedure which is a unique form of corporate effort to investigate and recommend action about problem colleagues. It is a quasi-formal

Table 5.1   Parallel findings in research in the United States and Britain

Freidson	*Rosenthal*
1 Collegial etiquette forbids criticism.	1 Professional norms and etiquette shape thinking about mistakes, competence and criticism.
2 Withdrawal of favours.	2 Changing referral patterns; marginalization.
3 'Talking to' in an educational manner.	3 The terribly quiet chat.
4 Confrontation handled by collective representatives.	4 Confrontation collective: chief of staff; LMC secretary or chair.
5 Turning tough cases over to administration.	5 Turning tough cases over to managers.
	6 Protective support.
	7 Three (now Four) Wise Men.

mechanism to enhance professional self-regulation, even if it does not work effectively all the time. The procedure has significant potential for being a useful tool if appropriately and skilfully used. It is the kind of corporate approach that Bosk finds lacking in American hospitals.[3]

Protective support is a well-known phenomenon in American hospitals and indeed, from anecdotal evidence, in many professions and work settings. Colleagues cover for colleagues when problems arise to keep work going, to keep institutions functioning, to help friends in need. More systematic research is needed to assess the impact of protective support over time, on the quality of work and on the individual being protected.

Another form of corporate action is found among GPs in Britain: corporate rejection in the form of being pushed out of a partnership. General Practice partners, dissatisfied with each other's work or personalities, can sever the relationship. This can preserve the reputation of the partnership or rid it of an incompatible doctor. It also has another consequence. It may push a weak doctor into a solo practice where there is even less opportunity for scrutiny of clinical work.

Swedish research

In 1990, when the research for the present study was completed in Britain, similar research was carried out in Sweden using the same research protocols. It was conducted in only one area of the country, albeit one similar to the two regions in Britain in that it included an urban academic medical centre and its catchment area. The same array of practitioners and managers were interviewed. This material, in its full form, will be rendered separately.

Swedish surgeons and GPs are both salaried employees of public bodies, the County Councils, which have major responsibility for financing and administering most health-care facilities. Like Britain, Sweden has a public health-care system supported by public funds. All Swedish doctors employed in the public sector have life contracts. One important difference in the job benefits of Swedish doctors is the possibility of receiving a full pension well before retirement age. Like Britain, the Swedish system is going through a series of changes to emphasize internal markets and various forms of privatization, with the same goal of improving efficiency, productivity, cost control and reducing public spending.

A brief overview of the Swedish cases reveals the following differences and similarities. First, in Sweden there is more separation between administrators and doctors, a more centralized administration working at greater remove from doctors. This results in more highly stratified information networks reducing access to information for administrators even more than in Britain; there is less sharing of 'gossip' between various groups.

Second, there is even greater reluctance to criticize, not only because of professional norms which are the same, but also because of cultural norms that discourage public criticism of anyone. Problem doctors are a 'forbidden' subject, a subject of shame that one of their numbers should be causing problems or found to be incompetent. The chief of a service who has to deal with the problem often feels alone and isolated in doing so because it is hard to speak to others about it.

Third, there is a tendency for protective support to be more common, more elaborate and somewhat easier to enact. There is, in general, more control over doctors' schedules. It is easier not to put a problem doctor on night or weekend duty, not to schedule the doctor for surgery. Nurses taking calls and making schedules refer patients to other doctors. It is particularly easy to do this in the primary care centres but also entirely possible in hospitals.

Finally, in Sweden job change is more common, sometimes in the form of 'exporting' the problem to another unit.

Other observations from the Swedish portion of the study suggest that the suspected alcoholic doctor may be even more tolerated because of general cultural drinking norms. There do not appear to be any more elaborate or effective mechanisms for dealing with this and other impairments, nor any easier ways of getting doctors to accept that they are impaired. Older 'problem' doctors are harder to deal with than younger ones. It is estimated that 5–10 per cent of the doctors in any region or district are problem doctors. And problem doctors are often thought to have been problem medical students.

It appears that the identification of problem doctors and the use of informal mechanisms are confounding and frustrating problems in Britain, Sweden and the United States. One can conjecture that it is confounding and frustrating in all societies.

The fact that doctors work in public systems, are salaried and have life contracts has stimulated more professional corporate effort in Britain and more system corporate effort in Sweden than in the USA. Into the 1990s, as British and Swedish medicine becomes more privatized, and American medicine more regulated, it is likely that the informal approaches, in the three countries, to problem doctors will converge.

All these countries would do better in coping with problem doctors if there were more research, more systematic attention and more professional training.

DISCUSSION

This research points to a number of observations and challenges. There is ample indication that informal mechanisms are preferable for many reasons that range from considerations of morale to conserving monetary and time resources and including individual and social investments in medical education. As in all social institutions and organizations, formal rules and procedures must exist as a last resort, as a declaration of possible use in extreme situations. But to use informal approaches for problems is more humane and less costly. To use informal approaches effectively, however, requires skill.

There are new opportunities and dangers in the changing NHS to work with problem doctors. While more powerful managers may bring greater attention to problem doctors, it is co-operation between managers and doctors and managerial support for colleagues trying to deal with colleagues that will be most effective for improving clinical work.

The challenges posed by the findings of this study include: first, learning how to assess troublesome behaviour more quickly to protect the patient, help the doctor and protect the work environment of the clinical unit; second, separating the various categories of 'incompetence' and 'problem' doctors and developing relevant, effective techniques appropriate to each without demoralizing the doctor whose problem may be temporary; third, understanding that the poor clinical work that may accrue from problem doctors is a subset of the larger, more important issue of medical mistakes and accidents in general; and finally, changing professional norms and etiquette in the face of growing and better information about clinical practice.

This study has provided a glimpse at the efforts of a small number of consultant surgeons, GPs and managers in the British NHS to regulate themselves in an informal manner. They are members of a profession that has long argued it should be free of outside regulation by virtue of its highly technical knowledge and its high sense of responsibility. As Freidson has noted, the profession sees itself as 'the sole source of competence to recognize deviant performance and to regulate itself in general. Its autonomy is justified and tested by its self-regulation.'[4]

The profession of medicine in Britain, as in many other countries, has been increasingly criticized for its unwillingness to discipline itself rigorously.[5] It will work hard to maintain self-regulation and its autonomy in the coming decade. To do that, it must understand its own informal mechanisms better and improve their effectiveness. It must also establish an entire system of comprehensive peer review.

Freidson observed, in one of his earliest discussions of the medical profession and its unique autonomy, how easily physicians neutralize outside control.[6] They now need 'an augmented collective spirit of service in order both to seek out and correct deviation without destroying discretion or commitment'.

There is an important relationship between the findings of this research and traditional professional norms concerning medical mistakes and accidents. It is clear that the ways in which doctors think about their work, its uncertainties and their fallibility and everything that follows from that, are most important in shaping their thoughts about accidents, mistakes and adverse events.

Yet there is growing empirical evidence that clinical practice may not be as uncertain as is generally believed. What does the systematic, empirical research reveal about the extent of medical accidents and errors and the ability of the profession to avoid them and about the ability of the profession of medicine to reduce the number of adverse events? And what does this evidence suggest about the transformation of traditional professional norms and etiquette?

6

EMPIRICAL RESEARCH ON MEDICAL MISHAPS AND MISTAKES: CHALLENGES TO PROFESSIONAL NORMS

In many activities . . . errors and accidents are the subject of systematic study . . . aircraft accidents are extensively investigated and extraordinary measures taken to minimize the risks of air travel. The risk of death under anaesthesia is comparable to the risk of accident on a commercial flight. Yet in anaesthesia and medicine generally, accidents are seldom discussed publicly and few studies are conducted. Many doctors review their work in morbidity and mortality meetings. This does not usually extend to systematic study and the results are not usually communicated to the wider medical community . . . research into medical accidents has been greatly neglected but can and should be studied.[1]

There is no question that the quality of care in the NHS is good and, in some specialty and geographic areas, excellent. And as medical science and art have improved since World War II, so has care in the NHS. However, improved research methods have permitted better understanding of adverse events in clinical practice in Britain and other countries.

A growing body of research has been undertaken in the last twenty years that provides insights into what are variously called medical mishaps, mistakes, errors and adverse events. While they vary in methodology, scope, rigour and unit of study, these studies contribute to a growing and deepening understanding of clinical practice and outcomes. Some of the research has been pioneered by the Department of Health with the royal colleges; some is the result of new conceptual ideas and research methods. A great deal is stimulated by mounting pressure for cost containment in health care and increases in clinical efficiency as well as recent concerns about medical malpractice litigation. Much of the research is conducted by medically trained professionals working with behavioural and social scientists.

THE WORK OF THE ROYAL COLLEGES AND THE DEPARTMENT OF HEALTH

The royal colleges have long been leaders in early versions of outcomes research. The first, and the oldest, are the confidential enquiries into maternal deaths conducted, since the first report for the years 1952–54, by the Department of Health, the Royal College of Obstetrics and national anaesthesiology associations.[2] These studies include a standard, systematic enquiry into every case of maternal death in Britain during pregnancy, delivery and puerperium. Since 1973, deaths associated with anaesthesia are also scrutinized. A senior consultant obstetrician assesses each record for the factors causing death and comments on avoidable factors. The records are subsequently reviewed in the Department and analysed in the context of a wide variety of medical and demographic factors. Strict confidentiality is observed at all levels.

The aggregated data are published and available publicly. The presence of an avoidable factor 'implies that there was some aspect of the mother's care which fell short of the ideal and may have contributed to the fatal outcome'.[3] A great deal of data are available in these studies. For example, in the 'Distribution of 347 avoidable factors in the series', 1970–72,[4] 42 per cent of avoidable deaths were attributed to the hospital obstetric staff; 30.5 per cent to the patient; 16.7 per cent to the general practitioner; 8.4 per cent to the anaesthetist; and 2 per cent to the midwife.

It is widely accepted that these confidential enquiries have contributed to a reduction in maternal mortality even while the avoidable factors have remained essentially the same. The last such enquiry was conducted in 1989.

THE WORK OF THE ROYAL COLLEGE OF PHYSICIANS (RCP)

The RCP, with the help of the King's Fund, set up a Medical Services Study Group in 1977 to promote research on the quality of clinical care among physicians.[5] The Group generated a number of studies such as 'Deaths under 50', 'Deaths from meningococcal infection' and studies in such areas as bronchial asthma, poisoning and diabetes. An effort has been made to emphasize avoidable mortality and morbidity. Meningococcal infection was chosen, for example, because considerable mortality persists despite a cure that has been known and available for forty years. This ongoing effort is concerned with improved data and data collection as well as spreading medical self-audit.

In another effort, the RCP established a national Working Party on Medical Audit which met for several years and proposed a system of audit in 1989 that the RCP would like to see its members and fellows adopt.[6] The document outlines a useful first-stage audit protocol which can be the basis for future development to more rigorous models. Since 1989, evidence of effective formal audit is sought by the RCP as a condition for the recognition and approval of training posts.

THE ROYAL COLLEGE OF GENERAL PRACTITIONERS

The RCGP has a long-established and ongoing series of quality assurance and audit projects often informed by the work of the international quality assurance theoretician Avedis Donabedian.[7] Its journal has published a series of articles about improving the patient care provided by general practitioners: quality assessment, audit of specific clinical practices (such as prescribing), prevention, symptom diagnosis, attitudes towards audit and incentives for instituting and improving audit.[8]

ROYAL COLLEGE OF SURGEONS AND CO-OPERATING ORGANIZATIONS: CONFIDENTIAL ENQUIRIES INTO POSTOPERATIVE DEATHS

The Confidential Enquiry into Postoperative Deaths (CEPOD) is another important and recent national study and audit carried out by an independent organization under the auspices of the Royal College of Surgeons, the Association of Anaesthetists, the Association of Surgeons and six other colleges and associations. The first report was published in 1990 and a second in 1992.[9] National outcomes data on surgical and post-surgical mortality rates, infection rates and wound complications are collected and subjected to statistical analysis to establish trends and norms. These studies explore correlates and causal factors and feed aggregated and anonymized information back to the specialty. The expectation is that such peer comparisons will inspire improvement in individual clinical practice.

The first CEPOD pointed to problems of incomplete records and data, inadequate emergency services, uneven supervision of junior staff, surgeons operating outside their specialty areas and low autopsy rates.[10] The findings of the second study also included these and added: questionable quality of locums, isolation of staff grade post surgeons, the strain of split work sites and deficiencies of operating department assistants and nurses.[11]

A comparison of the two studies reveals the extent to which surgical practices had improved after feedback of results from the first study. Necropsy rates improved as did consultant participation in operations and the presence of consultant anaesthesiologists, although they are still unlikely to be there in high risk emergency room (ER) operations.

Curiously, participation rates in the second study were down 20 per cent compared to the nearly universal participation of surgeons in the first CEPOD. The findings for individual surgeons suggest the need for better audit, clearer documentation, increased supervision of junior staff, staff grade posts and locums, and better liaison between surgeons, anaesthesiologists and pathologists. Despite the improvements documented, Nixon suggests: 'Overall, CEPOD does not seem to have stimulated a radical change in operative practice, but where movement has occurred, it is in the right direction.'[12] CEPOD has been criticized for its methodology. One relevant piece of research that could improve the accuracy of CEPOD appeared in 1992.[13] It describes and evaluates a post-operative community surveillance programme for the detection of wound complications after hernia operations. Community surveillance appears to provide a more accurate detection rate of wound complications after surgery. Complications were detected in 28 per cent of the patients with extended surveillance compared to only 7 per cent in the hospital case records of the same patients. 'Compilation rates after surgery are a reflection not only of the standards of surgical practice but also the rigour with which they are sought.'[14]

Despite the criticism of the CEPOD reports, one authority calls it 'the most ambitious audit undertaken in the United Kingdom, and the term "CEPOD" is now firmly established in the vocabulary of surgeons and anaesthetists'.[15]

ASSOCIATION OF ANAESTHETISTS OF GREAT BRITAIN AND IRELAND

Published in 1982 by the Nuffield Provincial Hospital Trust[16] and repeated, these series of studies on mortality associated with anaesthesiology sponsored by the professional association, establish the anaesthesia factors associated with mortality. These include the anaesthesia itself, inappropriate level of training of the anaesthesiologist, lack of appropriate equipment, inappropriate dosage of drugs, fluid overload and inadequate monitoring. The study found that 280 deaths per year were attributable to anaesthesiology and there were 1,800 deaths in which anaesthesiology played a part. One of the most striking conclusions of the study is that 'the events which caused these deaths have not changed much over the last thirty years'.[17] The study goes on to put these findings in perspective, pointing out that 'the process of anaesthesia is remarkably safe'.[18]

It may be noted that this specialty lends itself to relatively definitive scrutiny. It has taken responsibility for systematic self-scrutiny to identify problems and to feed back information to its practitioners, and has been doing this for over thirty years.

The issue seems to be getting practitioners to use such information to change clinical practice.

A WIDE VARIETY OF OTHER MEDICAL ACCIDENTS AND ERRORS RESEARCH

Overview of research on medical accidents in the UK

A 1989 article in the *British Medical Journal* argues that systematic study of medical accidents is a much neglected field compared to such studies in transportation and in industry.[19] Vincent points out that the general finding in all accident research is that human error complicated by organizational factors is the main cause of accidents. Further, he asserts that 'most accidents do not involve negligence'.

In his review of the medical accident literature, Vincent finds little in the way of scientific studies. 'Little is known about the overall incidence of medical accidents in the UK.' Extrapolating from a 1974 California study of medical accidents, he suggests that there may be 230,000 accidents yearly in the UK, 40,000 due to negligence. He notes that the confidential enquiries in obstetrics/ gynaecology, anaesthesia and surgery 'all found that a high proportion of deaths were avoidable'.[20]

While Vincent asserts that medical audits stop short of identifying mistakes (and that this is not their primary purpose), one unusual audit of the treatment of severe trauma identified missing or delayed diagnosis, and failure or inability to carry out treatment. Many studies indicate that errors in medicine are common but it is rare for them to pinpoint the cause of errors. He is particularly struck by the lack of systematic study of the impact of fatigue on junior doctors.

Looking at descriptive studies of medical accidents, Vincent points out that there are multiple contributory factors. These include: personal characeristics of the practitioner, transient states (caused by alcohol, drugs, fatigue and mood); patient characteristics (for example, the difficulty in interpreting test results from a patient with an established disease); and organizational factors such as overworked staff.

Vincent summarizes the results of some of his own studies on the Medical Protection Society records where it was possible to establish a pattern of 'deficiencies in training, supervision, clinical abilities, organizational factors and poor communication' as factors in medical accidents.[21]

The article ends with a series of recommendations: that medical audit systematically examine accidents and that major epidemiological and descriptive studies of medical accidents be conducted in the UK.

Medical Protection Society projects

A series of studies based on a retrospective review of cases in the files of the MPS and carried out by an academic research team have begun to appear. For example, a review of all anaesthetic and surgical cases involving a death, reported to the MPS between 1982 and 1986, was carried out by medically qualified assessors. Twenty per cent of the cases 'contained avoidable errors'.[22] In anaesthesia, the errors ranged from failed intubation, through problems with equipment, to unsupervised junior doctors. Failed communication of patient information between the two specialists was also noted. 'An important finding . . . was that avoidable deaths are rarely the result of a single major error but are frequently the end point of a cascading sequence of events.'[23]

Another MPS study reviewed 64 obstetric accident cases that came to litigation between 1983 and 1987. In most of these cases, three major areas emerged: mismanaged forceps; poor handling of electronic fetal monitoring information; and unsupervised junior doctors. While the number of cases is small, the authors contend the findings 'reflect more general problems: the ability of junior doctors to interpret fetal heart traces accurately, their ability to use forceps and the involvement of senior staff in running a labour ward and delivery suite'.[24]

Other obstetric research

A study of obstetric accidents from the patient's point of view was reported based on cases in the files of Action for Victims of Medical Accidents.[25] Cases included stillbirths, perinatal or neonatal death and long-term mental or physical handicap. Forty-one cases included a letter from the parent and an independent review by a senior obstetrician. The review's main criticisms were of inadequate fetal monitoring, lack of involvement of the senior staff and inadequate records. Women complained of being ignored, given too little information and never obtaining a clear explanation of their child's condition.

A 1990 study of decisions in obstetrics[26] studied the decision to use Caesarean section for the diagnosis of fetal distress in a teaching hospital over a 15-year period. Thirty per cent of the operations were found to be unnecessary. Further, it was found that there was substantial disagreement among the research auditors about whether a Caesarean section was called for in particular cases. And when faced with identical information at different times, the auditors were inconsistent 25 per cent of the time.

Surgical error

A recent article describing 646 orthopaedic surgeons in the NHS who have been sued, established the nature of the adverse events involved. These, ranked in order of frequency, are errors of surgical technique, problems of spinal surgery, junior staff errors, missed fractures and dislocations, wrong digit/side operation, among others. The causes of the accidents fall into two groups: technical (inexperience, inadequate help, forgetting safety procedures); and behavioural (communications failure, overconfidence, over-work).[27]

Problems in general practice

A review of a random selection of 1,000 GP complaints (made in 1982–89) from the data base of the Medical Defence Union, reveals 13 categories of criticism.[28] The most important category was failure to visit, and in a third of these cases the patient died. The second most common criticism was failure to diagnose, missed diagnosis or late diagnosis. The most common of these were appendicitis, ectopic pregnancy, perforated peptic ulcer, early pregnancy, myocardial infarction and carcinoma of the breast. The other categories of criticism, in order of importance, were failure in prescription, failure to arrange emergency admission and failure to examine. In a quarter of the cases, complainants were motivated by a desire to protect other patients.

Two hundred and eighteen general practices and their management of 1,775 asthma patients were studied to compare the actual management of asthma attacks with recommended guidelines.[29] Reported management was frequently at variance with recommended guidelines. In all grades of clinical severity, there was underuse of nebulized bronchodilators and systematic steroids. Maintenance therapy after an attack was often not practised. The authors of the study suggest that techniques for distributing guidelines be studied and improved.

Avoidable death research

Avoidable death research, by Walter Holland in Britain, has established extensive epidemiological data on patterns of avoidable deaths in large populations.[30] Holland has found that standardized mortality rates in different areas of England vary from 43 to 162 (per 100,000 inhabitants) for cervical cancer, from 19 to 250 for tuberculosis; between 31 and 249 for asthma; between 0 and 263 for rheumatic heart disease; from 0 to 379 for acute respiratory disease; and from 0 to 228 for appendicitis. It should be noted that similar differences were found between five EC countries. The reasons for the variations differ with the diagnostic category, but Holland suggests that the wide range includes a certain proportion of avoidable deaths in each diagnostic category.

The TRISS methodology was utilized to identify preventable trauma deaths in a retrospective study of 267 patients admitted to the A & E department of a teaching hospital during a one-year period. Of the 44 deaths, 25 (56.8 per cent) were found to have been preventable. The study includes a number of recommendations by a panel of six consultants who reviewed the preventable death cases.[31]

Avoidable death research has spread to include substantial international comparisons. The first *European Atlas of Avoidable Deaths* covered the period 1974–78 and the second has recently appeared.[32]

Shaw, in 1990, reviewed a wide variety of avoidable death research and described its increasing use epidemiologically and clinically as an indicator of quality. While he points out that many of the studies are technically weak or inadequate, he asserts this is minor compared with their usefulness, as long as their findings are translated into changes in local practice.[33]

British autopsy study

A 1992 autopsy study, reported in the *British Journal of Surgery*,[34] compared autopsy findings with clinical findings in 312 surgical patients. The primary clinical diagnosis was correct in 93 per cent of patients; complications had been correctly diagnosed in 60 per cent and error in treatment was found in 16 per cent. Error in treatment had an adverse impact on the course of disease in 11 per cent of the patients. The authors argue that autopsy is a valuable tool for surgical audit.

Junior doctors

A recent literature review on quality of care and junior doctors examines the effects of existing systems of medical staffing on quality of care in the NHS.[35] 'There is evidence that the existing system reduces the quality of care principally through mistakes associated with inadequate supervision, and lowered humanity of care due to tiredness.' Additional interviews with junior doctors find that the training value of nighttime work is low.

A set of articles appearing in the *British Medical Journal* in 1990[36] reviews the issue of stress in junior doctors. Lack of meaningful support as well as long hours are again noted as a problem affecting performance as well as morale. Studies of stress in female junior house officers indicate they can be more stressed than their male colleagues. The correlates of stress for all junior doctors – overwork, effects on personal life, serious treatment failures with their patients and talking to the distressed relatives of patients – can be further complicated by various forms of sexism.

A more recent discussion of stress and doctors at all stages of their careers appeared in a BMA report, 'Stress in the Medical Profession'.[37] This report points out that the many changes occurring simultaneously in the NHS are the cause of uncertainty and stress for many doctors who feel their role as clinicians is increasingly undermined by managers. The report finds that doctors report experiencing stress from medical school on, but are never taught the techniques of stress management. The report reviews the literature on stress and junior doctors and comments on the experience of GPs and consultants. The report calls for easily available stress counselling and a specialized occupational health service, pointing out that industry is more advanced in this regard.

A study of complaints in the Accident and Emergency department of a London hospital examined cases over a 33-month period. It is the view of the researchers that 'the errors and mistakes of diagnosis leading to complaints adjudged to be substantiated reflected inexperience of medical staff . . . and could only be avoided if more senior and experienced staff had been available'.[38]

City of Birmingham diagnostic errors

Perhaps one of the most startling findings about medical errors is the revelation that at least 42 patients at the bone tumour unit of the Royal Orthopaedic Hospital in Birmingham had their cases misdiagnosed and received extensive treatment when none was called for.[39]

Current enquiry is likely to uncover more erroneous diagnoses. Much of the blame for the errors is attributed to a consultant pathologist who is now said to have multiple sclerosis. One of the confounding aspects of an enquiry that was under way in September 1993 was that other doctors at the hospital had been aware of the errors in the pathology department for some time before they came to light.

RECENT RESEARCH FROM THE UNITED STATES

Medical outcomes and effectiveness research

The US government and American business which pay for most Americans' health insurance, have long been interested in how to contain health-care costs and at the same time, ensure quality of care. What has emerged as a major effort to combine these two goals is medical outcomes and effectiveness research and the establishment of clinical practice standards. The 1989 Omnibus Budget Reconciliation Act of the US Congress created the Agency for Health Care Policy and Research (AHCPR) to stimulate effectiveness research.[40]

Current outcomes research is inspired by studies that demonstrated geographic variation in style and delivery of medical care which seemed to be explained by medical management uncertainty.[41] Funded by the AHCPR and private foundations, outcomes research measures what happens to patients as a result of the treatment they receive, and often compares different treatments and treatment modalities. The number of studies in the USA (funded by the government) has grown from four in 1989 to 89 in 1993.[42] The President and Department of Health and Human Services are supporting a 23 per cent increase for the AHCPR budget for 1994, to a total of $130.3 million.[43]

Almost all effectiveness research projects funded by AHCPR are led by medical clinicians. Projects include[44] the management of infants and children with fever without source, primary care providers and the recognition and treatment of depression, cataract surgery, prostate cancer, type II diabetes, coronary care alternatives, pressure ulcer prevention, and pain management. These are just a few examples of the projects under way or completed. The studies become the basis for practice guidelines.

Two of America's leading medical clinics, Mayo and Cleveland, are providing their own contributions to medical outcomes and effectiveness research in a variety of areas.[45] Brain injury treatment, coronary artery disease, preoperative laboratory screening, methodologies for quality self-appraisal, and intensive care unit studies have appeared in the Mayo and Cleveland Clinic journals.

According to some medical leaders in the field, although clinical outcomes and effectiveness research has shortcomings,

it seems to be superior to the current peer review system because it encourages the development of a knowledge base and de-emphasizes punitive measures as a way to ensure quality and control costs. Patient outcomes research is an application of the science of medicine. Although the ability to measure patient outcomes in the near future is limited and much work must be done before an effectiveness initiative becomes clinically applicable, this initiative may result in improved quality of medical care at reduced costs. We suggest that the medical community embrace this research effort as part of its commitment to help patients and contribute to the well-being of society.[46]

Others state: 'Outcomes research is one of the most important tools policy makers, clinicians, managers and payers have to learn about the most effective and efficient ways to provide high quality care.'[47]

Outcomes research and related mechanisms are establishing themselves in Britain. A 1993 article in the *British Medical Journal*[48] suggests that guidelines for clinical practice that derive from outcomes research as well as guidelines for risk management, quality systems regulations and education 'are here to stay and will continue to be developed and used for educating and regulating the practice of doctors'.

The Harvard study of New York hospitals

The Harvard New York Hospital Injury Study,[49] looking at a random sample of all discharge records for 1984 in 51 New York State hospitals, identified injuries sustained by patients in the course of treatment and how many of them were the result of negligence. Of 31,329 medical records examined, 1,133 revealed an adverse event and 280 were the result of negligence. Extrapolating from these to all patient discharges from New York hospitals in 1984, the study concludes the following: for every 2.6 million people discharged, 56,000 sustained injuries with minimal impairment, 13,500 with moderate impairment, 3,800 with permanent impairment, 2,500 with permanent and total disabilities and 13,400 with adverse events that caused death.

While the 'negligent' adverse event occurred in 1 per cent of all hospitalizations, the number of individuals involved in a single year is substantial. Risk factors included age, severity of illness, race, type of insurance and the hospital where care was given. For example:

Adverse events rates varied 16-fold between hospitals and negligence rates varied from 0–70 percent. Twenty percent of operative adverse events were negligent; 75 percent of diagnostic mishaps were negligent; while only 2.9 percent of adverse events occurred in the ER, 70 percent of these were due to negligence.[50]

The study authors suggest that prevention efforts be directed to all adverse events, not just those that are negligent.

American house officers

A 1991 study of 114 American house officers (residents)[51] reports on a small, anonymous survey of house officer mistakes and responses to those mistakes. There were serious adverse outcomes in 90 per cent of reported cases, 31 per cent of which were death. Categorically, 31 per cent of errors were diagnostic, 29 per cent prescribing, 21 per cent evaluation, 5 per cent communications, and 11 per cent procedural complications.[52] The authors urge more active supervision of junior doctors, reduced work load, disclosure to patient and family (with the attending doctor). They suggest that these changes would help residents both reduce mistakes and learn more effectively from them.

Autopsy studies

A review of 47 years of published autopsy studies assesses the accuracy of clinical diagnoses through 50,000 autopsies of patients dying from one of 11 specific diseases.[53] Authored by pathologists from two American medical schools, the findings are used to discuss four issues: the accuracy of diagnoses; the change in accuracy over time; the impact of improved diagnostic equipment; and the probable existence of some degree of 'irreducible necessary fallibility' in the practice of medicine.

As for overall accuracy of diagnosis,

> there can be little question that a significant proportion . . . were misdiagnosed. Further it is physician factors rather than patient factors that account for the vast majority of missed diagnoses . . . with the misdiagnoses approximately evenly divided among errors of omission and errors of judgment . . .
>
> Lack of mental alertness or awareness on the part of the physician in attendance seemed to be a most common cause of diagnostic errors. More often than not, the correct diagnosis could have been made if the responsible physician had been less mentally stagnant about the problem.[54]

The autopsy studies reviewed indicate that recent diagnostic technology improvements 'have not had an apparent impact on the accuracy of clinical diagnosis among persons coming to autopsy'.[55] In fact, several studies indicate that overreliance on diagnostic testing can adversely affect diagnostic accuracy.

Finally, the authors suggest that their time-series data and further studies discover two realities: the uncovering of systematic faults that can be corrected, and the 'presence of an irreducible necessary

fallibility emanating from the uncertainty inherent in medical pre-
dictions based on human observations and the laws of natural
science'.[56] In other words, there is always a floor of unavoidable
adverse events in medicine, albeit a floor that may shift with time
and improved knowledge and skill.

Another, more recent autopsy study conducted by Professor Lee
Goldman of Harvard University claims that one out of five cases has
a missed diagnosis. In half the cases the correct diagnosis would
have saved the patient's life or prolonged it.[57]

Heart attack and treatment studies

A group of researchers from the New England Medical Center and
Tufts University School of Medicine studied the records of 5,773
ER patients with chest pain and other symptoms suggestive of
ischaemia. Of 1,050 patients with heart attacks, 20 (1.9 per cent)
were not diagnosed and five of the 20 died or suffered potentially
fatal complications. Among these patients who were sent home, the
doctor had missed ECG segment elevation or misinterpreted ECG
changes.[58]

Rand corporation studies, among others, have looked at the
appropriateness of treatment in a representative sample of Medicare heart patients in three states. The panel of review experts
found that 17 per cent of catheterizations were not necessary. A
similar study concluded that 20 per cent of pacemakers should not
have been implanted.[59]

Innovative medical error study

An innovative study of medical error was reported at a 1993
conference at Oxford University.[60] This study was jointly funded by
the Robert Wood Johnson Foundation and the American Bar
Association. Arguing the great difficulty in defining error or adverse event, and pointing out that the actual number of such events
in hospital care of patients is unknown, the study focused on a
variety of health-care workers in their daily contact with patients.
The researchers recorded what were called

> eyebrow-raising events: a situation in which someone in the
> hospital identifies a situation in which a health care worker
> undertook an action (or failed to undertake an action) when, at

the time, an alternate course of action was possible that the identifier felt was appropriate.[61]

The study covered a period from 1 July 1989 to 31 March 1990. The trained researchers attended rounds, nurse shift changes, conferences and other scheduled meetings to record these eyebrow-raising events. They recorded 2,318 such events for 1,047 patients. There were 'clear' indications of error in 48 per cent of the events; an additional 14.5 per cent were probable errors.

MINIMIZING MEDICAL MISTAKES: EXAMPLES FROM BOTH SIDES OF THE ATLANTIC

A small number of doctors have taken the leadership in discussing and promoting rigorous forms of audit and the analysis of error. For example, twenty years ago several British surgeons began advocating new forms of surgical audit. One of those surgeons is Professor Hugh Dudley (now emeritus) from London's St Mary's medical school. In a 1974 article in the *British Medical Journal*[62] he proposes a systematic method for the regular collection, study and analysis of patient data. He also suggests a rigorous system of analysis for diagnosis and treatment of selected conditions. Finally, he discusses an improved death and complications review that 'avoids disarming and self-serving admissions of guilt and misuse of uncertainty in medicine'. Such death and complications reviews, he says, 'combine to make the full scale deaths and complications audits in a surgical division as much a study in human behaviour as of the problems of patients'.

Dudley continues to call for 'critical self-audit' based on careful collection of data on all patients passing through a surgical department. He states such data can help 'remedy deficiencies in department priorities . . . evaluate clinical practices . . . contribute to clinical research . . . and is likely to benefit patients'. Dudley's work, formulated in computer software, represents 'short loop' feedback for getting remedial information back to surgeons in a short period of time.

A spate of books, written by doctors, is appearing in the USA which look on medical mishaps and medical uncertainty as a subject for close scrutiny and systematic improvement. One example is *Minimizing Medical Mistakes: The Art of Medical Decision Making*.[63] The author presents a well-thought-out, subtle but easy-to-follow schema for the processes of diagnosis and treatment and analysing what went wrong. In a chapter entitled 'Fallibility' he talks about undesirable results as either 'errors of ignorance' or 'bad outcomes'. The former require doing something about the ignorance. The latter, instead of the usual 'denial, discounting and distancing, call for recognizing, rectifying and resolving'. What this book represents is a growing recognition among the profession that there are systematic ways to practise, to detect patterns of practice and to review and improve one's clinical work.

DISCUSSION

Problem doctors and the empirical research

In terms of the subject of this book, it is interesting to note that none of the research particularly singles out specific categories of problem doctor other than overworked and undersupervised junior doctors. In point of fact, the issue is *general medical mistakes*, of which some problem doctors are a subset. We need specific research, if it is possible, to ascertain the errors and accidents of, for example, the impaired doctor.

It is likely that various forms of impairment bring various forms of impaired judgement. The recent incident at Birmingham Royal Orthopaedic Hospital appears to be the result of an ill doctor. Do all forms of impairment always impair all knowledge and all skills?

Where there are personality conflicts among experts, we have seen that there are accusations of incompetence, but this has also often turned out to be a clash of equally acceptable opinions. The empirical studies in general, however, are about medical work in general. And this has to be the larger overarching concern. Clearly there has to be more and better research in the whole area and a meta-analysis of large numbers of adverse events studies to provide an increasingly accurate picture of patterns of mistakes and accidents in various medical specialties.

The empirical evidence and professional thinking about medical mistakes

Extensive interviews with British Consultant surgeons and senior general practitioners reveal a widely shared set of perceptions about avoidable and unavoidable medical mistakes and mishaps. It is common for doctors to express a strong sense of permanent uncertainty about aspects of their clinical practice, to share a deep sense of personal vulnerability which makes it reasonable to understand and forgive colleagues who experience untoward patient outcomes. These powerful shared attitudes contribute to pervasive professional solidarity and strong norms of non-criticism particularly in front of the 'outside' world. These characteristics have been noted and discussed in some of the research and theoretical literature on the sociology of the medical profession, particularly by Eliot Freidson and Renee Fox.

They lead, logically, to the assertion that only the profession can judge the profession's work. These attitudes are modified when errors are gross and/or frequent, and when the practitioner in question has 'suspicious' characteristics, a difficult personality, a history of poor collegial interpersonal relationships, or signs of impairment. Otherwise, mishaps, mistakes and accidents are not generally the occasion for strong collegial sanctions of an informal or formal nature.

Some doctors among those interviewed express the view that their colleagues are too easy on each other and on themselves; that there are meaningful empirical studies of outcomes, accidents and mistakes that, if used systematically, could improve medical practice.

A small, selected sample of this growing body of research and evidence has been reviewed briefly in this chapter. It will take a meta-analysis of all such research to grasp the larger patterns. CEPOD I and II; maternal and infant mortality; anaesthesiology; reviews of 'unnecessary' deaths; documentation of errors and accidents; medical protection society research; variations in practice research; pathology and autopsy research – just this small selection of studies and enquiries suggests the following:

● The avoidable deaths enquiries that have been conducted for some decades have contributed to a reduction in avoidable deaths. However, those that remain are now clearly identified as caused by well-known factors that have not changed for decades. Other such research suggests that known knowledge is often overlooked in treatment of various illnesses and disease.
● Studies of junior doctors on both sides of the Atlantic indicate that fatigue and poor supervision contribute to junior doctor errors. This is particularly so in A & E departments.
● Autopsy studies on both sides of the Atlantic suggest a persistent rate of misdiagnosis and hence inappropriate treatment. New diagnostic technology may not improve diagnosis, according to the American study.

- There is increasing ability to point to different sources of adverse events: lack of knowledge, lack of skill, organizational problems, lack of communication among practitioners rather than intrinsic uncertainty in clinical practice.
- There is mounting evidence that educational material and the transfer of knowledge in continuing education sessions is not sufficient to get doctors to change and improve their clinical practice. Other techniques and incentives for change need to be developed.
- The most comprehensive study to date of adverse events in hospital populations (the Harvard study of New York State hospitals) suggests that incompetence and negligence are not as important as general mistakes and mishaps in injuring patients.
- Medical effectiveness and outcomes research provides increasingly useful information about which clinical techniques are most productive of positive outcomes. Outcomes research has its limitations and may not, in its current state of development, be applicable to all sub-specialties of medicine.

The growing interest and investment of resources in these types of research, promoted by a desire for more efficient use of resources and improved quality of care, promises to illuminate medical mishaps and mistakes with increasing accuracy.

Adjusting professional norms for the twenty-first century

The empirical research, now and as it improves, will necessarily challenge the general professional perception of permanent uncertainty and necessary fallibility.

It becomes imperative that the medical profession think in terms of *impermanent* uncertainty and *scrutinized* necessary fallibility. Research is shrinking the boundaries between the avoidable and the unavoidable. It begins to circumscribe understanding and forgiveness and restrict its universal and uncritical availability from colleagues. There will always be that shared sense of vulnerability among doctors, an important source of group solidarity and support. As research produces more evidence, and as more doctors understand and accept that evidence, the pressure will build, within the profession, for *less tolerance* of the avoidable, demanding (in the words of a professor of surgery) 'the scientific use of scientific evidence'. New medical technologies and knowledge will introduce *new parameters of avoidability*.

The study and feedback of information about medical accidents and mistakes will provide a continually shifting field of possibility for systematic improvement in the quality of medical care.

All these data now call for a comprehensive overall peer evaluation system and appropriate, effective incentives for use in continuous quality improvement.

7

COMING CHANGES: WILL THEY MAKE A DIFFERENCE?

We are confident that the new FHSAs . . . will bring improvements.
The new contracts will mandate audit and all the GPs will have to
participate. Although it is an early stage of audit, we are hopeful. Also,
there will be lower GP representation on the FHSAs (and less
domination). The government has been discussing medical audit with
the profession and feels that the profession as a whole has accepted
audit. The government now wants the production of outcome measures
and has been trying to get the profession interested in this. The
Secretary of State has invited all the presidents of the royal colleges to
talk about clinical standards.

(Department of Health official)

The doctors said the entire medical staff wanted to terminate him. Who
was I to question the entire staff? That hospital had always operated in a
'medical Mafia' way. The next thing that happened was that the health
authority offered him an astonishing buyout. I questioned that. The guy
wouldn't take the offer, and in the end lawyers were brought in. They did
reach a financial agreement and he's being paid to stay away. I have done
that. And the BMA is getting more keen on this. The old HC 61–112
procedure costs £200,000 and was very hard to use because facts will be
disputed. At the end the guy may appeal and get off.

(Regional Director of Public Health)

I know it is uncomfortable to speak ill of one's colleagues and I appreciate
that. But unless mistakes are highlighted, they won't be put right. They
must be put right. Looking at them early is a way of keeping standards
high; prevention is better than cure.

(Professor of surgery)

LOSS OF PUBLIC INNOCENCE: PATIENT COMPLAINT RESEARCH AND LITIGATION

My sister was on a GP's list. She went to him and he lost his temper. He was new and young. At the end of the session she asked for an ear cleaning. She complained of a bad pain after it was completed. Her brother-in-law was a doctor. Her ear-drum had been perforated. The GP said that it wasn't a problem. Our view was not necessarily the perforated ear-drum but his saying it was not a problem. This was negligence.

The issue was what to do about this GP. I insisted she see him and see if he was repentant but he blustered. She reported it to the FHSA and was asked to put it in writing; we helped her. It took weeks for a reply. And it was a bureaucratic reply: there was no case to answer, they are only concerned with the contracted service. We weren't having any of this; she wrote back saying I'll take it to a new level. This went on for three years and in the end, lawyers were brought in.

When it was obvious that we would go to court, it was sent to the NHS tribunal. They ruled that the doctor had been negligent and that the FHSA was at fault. My sister received a formal apology from the Minister of Health. The GP left practise and went into medical research. The FHSA got a letter of reprimand and my sister got a copy. She was satisfied. The whole thing took three years. Most people are not so persistent. Even my sister didn't know how to make the case.

The big message is: It's an absolutely closed system; it's extremely difficult to get into these issues. Nothing overt comes from the district. We know about the poor performance of the GMC – hopeless.

(Former Assistant District Nursing Officer)

Study of hospital complaints

Understanding complaints processes can illuminate not only why some complaints transform into claims, but also why for the overwhelming majority of complaints the possibility of a claim is virtually irrelevant; and why some who make claims insist they are not primarily interested in compensation, but in an explanation, apology or preventing the same thing from happening to others in the future.[1]

The number of complaints in the NHS has risen steadily in the last fifteen years. For example, according to government statistics, hospital complaints more than doubled between 1977 and 1991 from 15,112 to 32,996.[2] There is also evidence of the rise in complaints about GPs.[3] There have been striking increases in the number of claims and court cases.[4] In some NHS regions the number of claims and court cases equals the number of those in some states in the USA. Figures from the Medical Defence Union indicate that the MDU paid £30 million in claims and settlements in 1987 and £50 million in 1990.[5] Such evidence suggests a more emboldened public, less willing to accept the authority of the medical profession and more willing to express grievances and concerns.

Current research provides insight into the motivation of those who complain.[6] Based on a systematic study of one year's formal hospital complaints in two health districts, the research established that hospital complaints, including matters of a serious clinical nature, had clear goals. The overwhelming majority of those registering complaints wanted further information or treatment or wanted improvements for the future. Very few such complainants went on to institute claims although 30 per cent of the cases involved allegations of physical harm. The study also reviewed formal claims to the two health districts. Of these, only 13 per cent began as complaints; '87 per cent of claims did not pass through the formal complaints machinery at all'.[7] Research from the USA reveals similar patterns of two almost entirely different populations of patients, those who use the complaints machinery and those who bring legal claims.[8]

Some of the most comprehensive research about complaints against GPs suggests that, despite growing numbers, a very small percentage of the population actually complain about GP services, under 1 per cent, and 'probably 30 percent could be about competence'.[9] The Family Practitioner Committee complaints review process has focused on breaches of contract, not competence. According to Alsop:

> The technical competence of doctors is not questioned unless normative rules of behaviour are broken. Those who breach the norms get the severest fines, like fraud which is considered the worst offence. The FHSAs don't know what to do with incompetent doctors. Although the FHSA has the power to call an NHS Tribunal, it has to do so at its own expense.
>
> (Alsop 1990)

Alsop's research finds that the percentage of GPs found in breach of contract has doubled in ten years in some FHSAs. She also notes that FHSA–MSC meetings are often run as dispute not disciplinary hearings and that FHSA–MSC members have no training for their work.

The new FHSAs which replaced the FPCs in 1992, have enhanced disciplinary powers. Medical audit will also be required. It remains to be seen how the new disciplinary functions work in practice and how rigorous the medical audit instruments and committees are. The new medical audit efforts are discussed in detail below. Alsop asserts that more can be learned about the quality of GP clinical practice from complaints than from current medical audit instruments.

Linking all this research with the rise in the number of complaints suggests that while patients in the NHS are more likely to complain than ever before, their motivation is not for legal redress but other kinds of recognition of their grievance and of the problem. And they may be increasingly restless with review mechanisms that ignore possible incompetence.

As for the number of claims, the research suggests that these are rising.[10] Subscription rates for individual doctors tripled between 1986 and 1988. With the threat of risk-related premiums, the profession and the NHS agreed to institute Crown Indemnity, whereby the districts become financially responsible for claims and settlements involving their hospital doctors.

These trends and other studies suggest that the British public is changing; that there has been a loss of public innocence about medical authority and medical practice; that the public wants more information and more communication from the medical profession; that the public will increasingly seek partnership in the medical encounter and ask for more accountability from its doctors.

CHANGES IN THE NATIONAL HEALTH SERVICE

A number of reforms proposed in the government White Paper, *Working for Patients*,[11] have now become law by an Act of Parliament. Adapting the ideas of the American economist Alain Enthovan, the NHS is being reshaped. While it remains financed primarily out of public funds with access a right of citizenship, it will operate as an 'internal competitive market' with districts acting as purchasers of service. The hope is that this form of regulated competition will engender more efficiency, productivity and a higher quality of care.

In preparation for the internal market, hospitals meeting certain criteria are becoming self-governing NHS trusts with the ability to handle their own budgets and contracts with individual doctors. Large GP practices can become 'fund-holders' on the model of some American health-maintenance organizations, purchasing specialist services for their patients as deemed necessary.

Other changes include a devolution of responsibility from region to district to hospital; creation of new consultant posts; the reform of management bodies along 'business' lines; and the extension of medical audit by peer review will be extended throughout the NHS.

There will be an effort to build a closer relationship between the NHS and the private sector. Districts can use NHS funds to purchase private care. Competitive bidding will continue for support services and extend to clinical services. Joint ventures between the public and private sectors will be encouraged.

Another important element of the current reform is an increase in the role and authority of managers.

From administrator to manager: the empowerment of NHS management

From Thatcher to Major, the government has made greater empowerment of NHS managers on all levels a long-term goal. Beginning with the Griffith Report in 1983,[12] which called for a 'managerial culture' and held up managerial models from the business world for emulation, the system has moved towards transforming the old NHS administrative structure and style to one of efficiency-oriented management. The Griffith Report led to the creation of general managers at every tier of the NHS, with an emphasis on local decision-making. However, a single line of command, from the NHS general manager to the local unit manager, has been established. These managers, unlike the old management team administrators, have wider-ranging responsibility for their units. Performance indicators, performance reviews, cost assessment and extensive managerial training have all entered the NHS. Since managers are regarded as skilled professionals in their own right, people with managerial experience in business, industry and the military as well as former NHS administrators have been hired to fill the unit positions.

One of the seven key proposals in *Working for Patients* as the basis for changes in the NHS in the 1990s points to further refinements of the NHS managers' role: 'To improve the effectiveness of NHS management, regional, district and family practitioner management bodies will be reduced in size and reformed on business lines.'[13]

Expressions of such change are reflected in many of the interview statements of managers in the study described in this book. NHS managerial change has also been discussed widely in the professional journals and reports.[14] Best, in an assessment of what the new managerial initiatives are supposed to accomplish,[15] talks about more sophisticated training for the pragmatic realities of trade-off in the NHS, encouragement of innovation, attracting private sector resources into the NHS, balancing central managerial leadership with local discretion to make the best use of limited resources in the NHS.

Other analyses and studies of managerial change, of which there have been many, point to the difficulties in instituting such changes in well-established institutions like the NHS. The following highlights the not unexpected stumbling blocks to change:

> Griffith, for all its radicalism, was only a partial break from the past. There was now a chain of command which reached from the top to the bottom of the organization. There was also a new headquarters staff with a potential flexibility to match the exigencies of local need and form. But the Service was still strapped, for general managers at least, within a national strait-jacket. Local initiative was frustrated by ministers, civil servants, by supervisory management tiers and by powerful professional bodies. Doctors still gave orders . . .[16]

Some of these problems are reflected in a recent book written to train managers:

> This is going to be complicated in many cases by the very wide difference in experience and seniority between Consultants and the local managers with whom they come into contact. The average Consultant is going to be a man or woman in their 40s or 50s who has already been a doctor for 15 to 20 years. The average unit general manager is likely to be a man in his 20s or 30s with relatively few years of general management experience. From the Consultant's point of view, the average UGM is simply a bright lad who knows nothing about medicine and appears to be indifferent to the requirements of treating the sick. To the average UGM, the Consultant is an elderly self-satisfied gentleman, quite intolerant of well meant suggestions and absolutely resistant to change.[17]

Another point of view is expressed by one of the new unit managers in an academic hospital who was interviewed for this study. This manager is optimistic about the younger doctors and their relationship to managers.

> They are more open about medical audit, more inclined to be open to scrutiny, more willing to criticize each other. I've had more dialogue with the newer generation than with the old.

The younger consultants are taking audit on board while the older ones aren't so keen. There is a big resource crunch right now and the younger doctors are more willing to discuss what to keep and what to let go. They are more politically aware of management and prepared to share the difficult decisions. They are also less prepared to accept inappropriate behaviour from their colleagues.

This manager feels that medical audit will catch the incompetent doctor and that the new purchasing contracts will have to detail outcomes.

This will help reduce incompetence. Once the purchasing contracts are in place, we will have to demonstrate that we can do the job better than anyone else.

And there is also the public. They are demanding more information and they have more knowledge. They watch TV and they are more willing to litigate. This will have an impact as well. Finally, the new consultant contracts under the White Paper will strengthen the managers.

I am also enthusiastic about the new consultant-manager arrangements in this hospital. The Surgical Directorate has one foot in management and one foot in medicine. It is headed by a clinician who is expected to do management work which will include dealing with incompetence.

Crown Indemnity

On 1 January 1990 the government announced that all hospital and community doctors would be indemnified by their health authorities in a scheme known as Crown Indemnity.[18] Instead of purchasing indemnity insurance on an individual basis, authorities will cover this as well as new and existing claims of medical negligence and awards. This was the result of negotiations between the government and the professional pay review body which agreed that it would be unwise to take account of the rising subscription rates through pay and pension increases. Regions were urged to form pooling arrangements for large awards; coverage is to come out of authority budgets. Trust hospitals must cover themselves.

The advantages of Crown Indemnity, according to the Department of Health, include avoidance of differential subscription rates, automatic coverage of GPs and part-time staff doing hospital work, quicker settlements for patients, administrative simplification and financial savings.[19] Others suggest increased costs to authorities, lack of adequate legal resources for the health authorities and expedience in early settlement of claims.[20]

It has been suggested that doctors will become more accountable to their health authorities under Crown Indemnity,[21] which can discipline a doctor who proves costly or demand recompense for awards the district has paid out. The solicitor for the West Midlands Regional Health Authority has written an agreement contract between the regions and its districts that will permit him to 'recover' damages paid out where an incompetent doctor is involved.[22] Whether Crown Indemnity will eventually be used in this fashion or not remains to be seen, but it suggests a change in the relationship between health authorities and the doctors who work for them.

One of the hospital unit managers expresses the potential in this way:

> If it [Crown Indemnity] is going to be granted to the hospitals, then I want to be involved in the selection of the consultants and I want to hold their contracts. Things are moving in that direction; it is inevitable in two or three years. At the moment, payments out because of negligence cases will mean there will have to be a reduction of services. The district will be held liable for up to £300,000 – that's half a ward's budget. We are developing medical audit approaches, particularly in surgery and ob/gyn; the doctors are asking for it themselves and this is a good sign.

New opportunities for general practice and the FHSAs

A spate of articles in the last five years have analysed the changes, stresses and opportunities for general practice in the reformed NHS which, in addition to other reforms, would like to put more emphasis on community care. Donald Irvine's discussion in a 1993 issue of the *British Journal of General Practice* captures a wide range of the issues.[23]

Stressing the new opportunities that accrue from the new reforms, Irvine emphasizes the need to 'ensure that every practice provides a quality service which patients need and want, and which gives the taxpayer value for money'. Pointing to the international and NHS trends of demonstrating clinical effectiveness, rising consumerism, strengthened management, explicit practice guidelines, interdisciplinary teamwork and the pursuit of quality, calls for such things as quality assurance improvements focusing on outcomes, experimentation with different forms of GP contracts including traditional, unconventional and salaried GPs, improved continuing education for GPs that includes motivation for continuous learning and linkage to quality assurance activities, and improved approaches to accreditation and reaccreditation.

Irvine's paper is a call to general practitioners to 'put their own stamp on the new developments and so vigorously lead change in ways that will benefit both patient and health professionals'.[24] This article is a manifesto for general practice to embrace a number of mechanisms to improve the way it trains and regulates itself.

The Family Practitioner Councils which managed GP contracts have now been reconstituted as Family Health Services Authorities. The FHSAs have been strengthened in a variety of ways including the creation of chief executive posts that are accountable to the regional health authority. The FHSAs will supervise GP audit activities and manage the budgets for GP prescribing. There will be fewer GP representatives on the FHSA complaints review committees. Overall, FHSAs will have more official powers; how and to what end these are exercised depends on the skills and vision of the new chief executives.

Medical audit

While medical audit activities have been growing on a voluntary basis in the NHS, medical audit is now mandated as part of all doctors' contracts and will take place in all units in all districts. There is much discussion of the strengths and weaknesses of the audit process as now envisioned.

And there is considerable political interest in its development. Part of the pressure from the profession for audit may be due to the view that self-regulation is preferable to an imposed external system.[25] Indeed, in 1988 Mrs Currie (Minister for Health) stated: 'either doctors monitor their own performance . . . or someone else will do it for them'.[26] Medical audit is the 'systematic, critical analysis of the quality of medical care' by doctors in hospitals and in the community. It includes the analysis of procedures used for diagnosis and treatment, the use of resources and the resulting outcome and quality of life for the patient.[27] Audit should be a continuous cycle involving observing practice, setting standards, comparing practice with standards, implementing change and observing the new practice.

Working for Patients sets out the organizational procedures; it emphasizes the primacy of professional leadership but believes that management has a significant part to play in ensuring that the system of medical audit is effective. Hospital and community services district medical audit advisory committees chaired by a senior clinician have been in place since April 1991. Their remit is to plan and monitor the medical audit programmes and to produce an annual report; if necessary the district general manager can ask them to review a particular service. A similar committee at regional level will support local initiatives, organize audit of smaller specialties across the region, and arrange external peer review of problems that arise in districts. Ultimately the goal is to develop agreed objective criteria of a successful outcome.

'All general practices are to be involved in medical audit within three years [by 1992]; they will be overseen by a medical audit advisory group of each family practitioner committee consisting of doctors and "other staff", with functions broadly similar to those of the district committees, with which there will be cross representation.'[28] The HMSO report states that contracts of both consultants and GPs will be amended to include a requirement to participate in medical audit.

Four different approaches have been found to be useful for auditing clinical systems, with the type and amount of information available influencing the approach which is adopted.[29] The first approach is case note review, with feedback of results. This is one of the methods favoured by the Royal College of Physicians. Using this method it may ultimately be possible to develop agreed objective criteria of a successful outcome. This would usually involve the use of techniques for achieving agreement such as consensus conferences. The use of case note review would require an improvement in the quality of notes taken. Secondly, one could analyse routinely collected health service data. The recommendations of Korner regarding the amount and type of health service information which should be collected will aid this approach. Thirdly, population-based epidemiological studies could be conducted, to overcome the problem of only auditing hospital patients who may have been selected into treatment. Finally, an analysis of the appropriate use of investigations and therapies could be undertaken. Such an analysis has been carried out, and guidelines produced, in a number of fields including: the use of preoperative chest X-rays; the number of laboratory tests conducted; and the use of cervical lymph node biopsy. There are examples of all four approaches functioning in the NHS.[30]

As already reviewed in Chapter 6, a number of audit projects were well under way before the new contracts. But progress is considered to be relatively slow. There are a number of reasons for the lack of progress of audit in the NHS. Some clinicians argue that audit is implicit and is already being carried out. This presupposes that current practice is correct, although many routine procedures have never been evaluated. The term 'audit' is sometimes regarded as threatening. The Medical Audit Working Party of the Royal College of Physicians spent much time trying to find a less emotive alternative – for example, 'clinical review', 'quality assurance' or 'peer review'. But it concluded that medical audit was direct, easily understood and already in use.[31]

A further concern regarding audit is that since medical practice is complex, the defining of medical standards or developing a best documented practice is a very complicated and ever-changing process.[32] Indeed, it has been suggested that since no two surgical units are alike, it is not possible to argue from the figures of one to those of another.[33]

The time required to perform audit has also been given as a reason for not doing it.[34] In the UK the number of consultants in relation to the population served is considerably lower than in other countries which perform audit more extensively. McKee suggests that audit can be carried out despite this constraint, perhaps by redesigning summaries so that audit data are produced as a by-product, and by using a microcomputer.

However, McKee also state that there must be a recognition that audit takes time which will not be available for other activities (and it will require adequate clerical support).[35] Indeed, the government has stated that this issue of time to undertake audit will be dealt with in doctors' contracts.

However, Axton points out that 'it is difficult to see where extra time could be found in the average Consultant's day'. Audit will also require money. The government has set aside a central fund of a £¼ million to pay for audit, but this is considered to be an inadequate sum.[36] A further concern about audit is that it could threaten clinical freedom by political or bureaucratic intervention.[37]

Working for Patients states that management must be included in audit procedures, with full access to results, and have the power to initiate audits, usually involving some external peer review. Considerable pressure might be put on clinicians through this means. Thrifty managers may compare the costs of procedures in their respective districts and may be tempted to initiate audits based purely on financial constraints.[38] Furthermore, audit might discourage doctors from undertaking difficult but essential clinical work where there is a known element of risk.[39]

The question of confidentiality has also been raised with the issue of audit. Balfour suggests that 'there will need to be safeguards to protect surgeons from the consequences of plain speaking'. The working paper does stress the confidentiality of individual doctor's clinical judgments.[40]

Other criticisms of audit include the belief that the poor quality of information will be a barrier to effective audit, that audit substitutes for taking action; that staff could make more productive use of their time, and that it masquerades as research.[41] (Although McKee states that audit is now accepted as a valid form of research.) It has also been suggested that audit is unlikely to influence clinical behaviour.

Anderson *et al.* examined the prescribing of Dioxin, and developed a protocol using these data.[42] This protocol was distributed and discussed with all participating GPs. A year later a similar analysis was undertaken. Anderson *et al.* discovered that such unsolicited feedback of clinical information from a pooled survey is unlikely to influence clinical behaviour, at least over one year. Record-keeping had improved significantly in the group of principals carrying out the audit, but not the other principals in these practices. Thus Anderson *et al.* state that 'audit may only change the auditors'.

McKee states that it is important that audit is professionally led; this was emphasized in the 1989 HMSO White Paper. McKee also emphasizes the importance of dialogue between clinicians and management, in order to eliminate misunderstanding about the function of audit. He states that the clinicians and management must agree that the prime objective of audit is to improve patient care, and not to reduce costs regardless of quality of service. The proposed district medical audit advisory committees will enable this dialogue to take place.[43]

Overall it is clear that some see audit as a panacea for improving the quality of care in the NHS; others are less sanguine.

An early audit of audits in Oxfordshire 'disclosed considerable deficiencies in the process of practice audits'.[44] Another study, of surgical audit, raises questions about 'the problems of presenting and interpreting audit data'.[45] Many more studies are appearing and will appear that evaluate audit activities as they emerge in the 1990s. They will no doubt be informed by studies like *The Reliability of Peer Assessments: A Literature Review* which asserts that:

> research on quality assessment needs to be directed at modifying
> the peer review process to improve its reliability or at identifying
> indices not involving peer review that have sufficient validity

and reliability that they can be employed as independent measures of quality.[46]

Another ongoing issue is how to persuade practitioners to change clinical practice. Horder *et al.* have reviewed the literature on influencing GPs to change and improve clinical practice. They conclude:

> Although change is always occurring, its deliberate induce-ment and direction is usually slow and laborious. Doubt is cast on the efficacy of financial incentives and of unsolicited feedback about performance. Evidence for the influence of audit on behaviour is so far small. By contrast, personal contact with doctors, nurses, and other colleagues and to a lesser extent with patients is relatively effective whether in the teamwork of practice or in more formal education. But it is in the combining of different methods which brings the most success in influencing General Practitioners.[47]

CHANGES IN PROFESSIONAL ORGANIZATIONS: NEW GMC PERFORMANCE MECHANISMS

The General Medical Council is seeking an amendment to the Medical Act of 1983 to broaden its professional regulatory powers. Its proposal will be considered by Parliament in 1994. After three years of study, the GMC now recognizes that it must accept complaints about professional performance. It will surprise some that the GMC has not considered this among its disciplinary responsibilities to date. But these have been limited, since the first Medical Act, to professional conduct. As expressed by Sir Robert Kilpatrick, president of the GMC:

> However, the GMC has been increasingly aware that there is a considerable gap in its present powers; at present it has no powers to conduct investigations into the day-to-day standard of professional performance of individual doctors, even though there may be evidence that a doctor's performance is seriously deficient and is placing patients at risk. Performance in this context means the standard of professional knowledge and skills which doctors usually display and his or her professional attitudes. The existing procedures of the GMC concerning

conduct or health are not sufficiently flexible to allow the GMC to investigate such matters.[48]

Kilpatrick goes on to point out there are no mechanisms to ensure that a doctor seeks retraining; and no mechanisms for measuring improvement. Now recognizing these deficiencies, the GMC will seek to remedy them by proposing changes to the Medical Act that create new powers to take on complaints concerning professional performance – that is, complaints about knowledge and skills – and request that they now be part of its formally designated responsibilities.

These procedures will be activated only with a complaint about a consistently deficient performance. The purpose of the new procedure is not to punish but 'to improve performance through counselling and retraining'. The proposed process, in its current version, would involve initial screening of the complaint by an MD member of the GMC to determine if the problem is one of poor performance, misconduct or ill health or some combination of these. In the cases calling for action, assessment would be made by a local committee of two same-specialty MDs and a non-medical assessor. Recommendations for counselling, remedial action and/or restrictions would be made. Reassessment at a suitable time that indicates satisfactory results would mitigate any further GMC action. Only a doctor who failed to co-operate or failed to improve would face formal proceedings before the new GMC Professional Performance Committee which would have power to suspend or restrict registration.

These proposals for professional performance review are not without criticism.[49] Questions are raised about how the distinction between performance and conduct will be made and the ability of the complainant to challenge assignment of a complaint; there is scepticism about the increased powers of the preliminary screener, the lack of post-disciplinary ability to conduct a performance review on the accused doctor's practice; there is the observation that the new procedures are similar to the old RMO clinical complaints procedure which has been roundly criticized by consumer organizations. It is pointed out that there is no commitment to speeding up a now lengthy set of procedures and there are some concerns about questions of confidentiality. From the perspective of this study, the proposed professional performance procedure is a combination of several existing but inconsistently applied informal and quasi-formal mechanisms that are cited in a number of cases reported in this book: the Three Wise Men and the efforts of some of the

RDPHs at retraining, the quiet talk. Administrative suspension has been a functional equivalent of the GMC power to suspend, of course without the complete removal of registration.

The GMC proposal is an encouraging step towards the kind of peer review that ought to be a part of the ongoing systematic activity of every local clinical unit. It is encouraging to see the GMC take this initiative to include clinical performance with ill health and professional conduct as appropriate areas of responsibility. However, based on the research described in this book, one may anticipate several problems.

It is clear that counselling and remedial action work with selected problem doctors. Assuming that impaired doctors are referred to the GMC Health Committee, this leaves personality problems, knowledge-deficient doctors and doctors who fail to keep up. The thrust of the new GMC proposal is a humane one: to try and help a doctor return to acceptable practice, to save the investment in a medical education, to save a career. It is not clear that the threat of procedural action is what will accomplish these goals. Deeper knowledge of the various kinds of problem doctor, the dynamics of their problems, known effective solutions, and known frustrations have to be studied more carefully.

Promoting local responsibility with incentives for such peer review is essential as the GMC sees only the tip of the iceberg. While the GMC is to be lauded for taking this important step to fill a 'major lacuna in the medical profession's procedures for self-regulation',[50] it can serve the profession and the public even more by actively supporting clinical outcomes and effectiveness research and continuous quality review and improvement.

The 1993 Birmingham case alone indicates that some improvement in the system is badly needed. There are those among the British medical profession who are leaders in this effort already.

WILL THE CHANGES MAKE A DIFFERENCE?

Theoretically, a number of these changes should have an impact on 'problem' doctors. The decline of life contracts in trust hospitals and elsewhere should make it easier to take appropriate action more quickly. Theoretically, medical audit should provide information for more rapid detection of problems. Theoretically, the new GMC performance review should serve as an alert to the profession that its leading professional body is deeply concerned with issues of competence. Theoretically, empowered managers should have broader tools for working with problem doctors. Theoretically, Crown Indemnity should provide incentives for districts and regions to work more vigorously to reduce medical error, assist impaired doctors and sort out personality conflicts. Theoretically, more assertive consumers should make it increasingly difficult to hide behind medical authority.

What seems theoretically possible does not necessarily happen in reality. All of these changes are important steps. What they can produce should not be overestimated. Evidence suggests that only if they are seen as early efforts in a continuing, consistent and creative process at improvement will they be effective. Empowered managers still need to get along with powerful doctors. Crown Indemnity cannot be a bludgeon that undermines trust in NHS care but rather a tool for identifying and improving possibly poor care.

There remain many accepted risks in medical care that can produce adverse events. But these risks need to be scrutinized more rigorously and consistently. Medical audit, in its current forms, is focused on the structure and process of medical care; it should be a stepping-stone to a focus on outcomes and effectiveness. Assertive consumers need to be transformed into active partners in diagnosis and treatment, not enemies and adversaries.

All of the royal colleges have taken steps to encourage some form of medical audit among their members; many continue their national surveys of avoidable complications and deaths. The next step for the royal colleges is to promote clinical effectiveness and outcomes research that can be tied to the promotion of clinical standards.

There is growing interest in the UK in its own versions of clinical outcomes and effectiveness research, the establishment of practice guidelines, risk management and other techniques for helping the profession review and improve its clinical work on a rigorous and ongoing basis.

The establishment of practice standards that are realistic for the average practitioner is preferable to standards that are unrealistic to reach. Unless a guideline accurately reflects the routine working practices of most doctors it will act only as a gold standard to be admired. Rather it should be an explanation of unsatisfactory practices, a plea for better coordination and a blueprint for simple measures to improve the state of affairs. Perhaps doctors need to be less idealistic and more honest about their present working conditions in order to describe the guidelines to which their practice conforms.[51]

Such systems will only work if there is a strong devotion to them on the part of the medical profession. Their expertise and commitment to various forms of peer review and medical audit are essential to make it effective and pervasive. In his speech on clinical freedom, Sir Raymond Hoffenberg, former president of the Royal College of Physicians, states:

> Would our professional freedom not be better preserved if we relied less on the courts and more on our own efforts to monitor and improve our standards? If we are to be accountable – and I most firmly believe we should be – would it not be preferable for us to account to ourselves?[52]

The royal colleges can lead the way in these efforts and also in the development of techniques and incentives to encourage doctors to take on new knowledge and continuously improve their clinical practices.

LONG-TERM IMPROVEMENT: A NEW APPROACH TO SELF- AND PEER REVIEW FOR THE PROFESSION

What are the implications of this research for the future of quality assurance in medical care, particularly as it relates to self-regulation and peer review?

It is clear from the collected cases that were successful, that the human and institutional costs are considerably less when the incompetent doctor is dealt with informally. It is less damaging to individuals and to institutions. It preserves the quality of interpersonal relationships; it provides a humane model for others in the organization. The problem is that the informal mechanisms are not successful in the majority of cases. How can they be strengthened?

There are a number of ways in which the informal mechanisms can be strengthened and made part of a comprehensive overall peer evaluation system that may be envisioned for the future.

First, how can the current informal efforts be improved?

1 *Training.* The field of human resource development has accumulated considerable knowledge about impaired personnel, from the alcoholic to the mentally unstable. It has also developed a repertoire of techniques for identifying and helping impaired personnel. The same is true for the 'difficult' personality. Introduction to these should be part of the standard training of medical leadership in every health- and medical care delivery

unit. Organizations such as the Physicians Health Foundation of the American Medical Association which co-sponsors (with the Canadian Medical Association and Canadian and US federations of State Licensing Boards) international conferences on physician health now provide timely information. All sorts of resources exist for other categories of problem doctor.

2 *Easily-implemented job alternatives.* There should be a well-accepted set of options including mini-sabbaticals, leave for continuing education, re-education and re-employment that are easily implemented. Leave and sabbaticals should be regarded as desirable to eliminate any stigma attached to them. The Department of Health has already encouraged the development of these.[53]

3 *Early training for self-insight and co-operation.* From the cases collected, it is clear that many doctors are unable to accept criticism or admit problems. During the medical education process, there should be frank and open discussion of the problem doctor and the inculcation of a norm of self-appraisal (along with a norm of lifelong peer review) so that doctors will not resist the admission of impairment or problems of competence. This may be likened to the norms of rapid report of technical errors that Bosk describes in the training of surgical residents.

4 *The development of organizational incentives and support for using the informal mechanism.* Release time, expert support, easily obtained temporary replacements, automatic leave and sabbaticals, and personal expert counselling services should be in place and well known, to support the use of informal mechanisms. They should not be left to operate on an *ad hoc* basis.

A COMPREHENSIVE OVERALL PEER EVALUATION SYSTEM

However, these approaches alone are not sufficient. We can envision a comprehensive overall peer evaluation system that begins with the medical school admissions process and continues until retirement. What would such a system include?

1 A more sophisticated medical school selection process that identifies the 'difficult' personality and the problem prone.
2 A commitment on the part of the medical schools to 'counsel' students with emerging problems into the most appropriate specialties or out of the field of clinical medicine.

3 Teaching and socializing a commitment to ongoing medical audit and peer review and self-scrutiny as a lifelong commitment of each individual doctor. Teaching stress management techniques.

4 More rigorous and systematic supervision of junior doctors that includes reduction of working hours to more realistic levels.

5 The institution of meaningful peer review mechanisms in every health-care delivery unit, mechanisms that are more rigorous than those that exist today at their best; mechanisms that are a routine part of daily practice.

6 Support for regional centres of aggregated peer review data and clinical outcomes research to which every clinician gives and from which every clinician receives data. Such centres would work to narrow the differences of opinion about diagnosis and treatment that exist between equal experts.

7 Support for the informal coping mechanisms as listed above; clearer delineation of responsibility for problem GPs between the LMC and the FHSA and in the hospitals; more co-ordination of information and well-defined problem management techniques and time frames.

8 Professional training about management of problem doctors for the Four Wise Men and for medical managers.

9 Incentives for earlier detection and help for impaired doctors (thus avoiding, for example, the Birmingham case).

10 Development of contracts that take potential problems into account by enumerating problems that are known to emerge, what informal mechanisms will be used, the help that will be offered to doctors with problems, and the formal mechanisms for suspending or ending contracts that exist.

11 A series of incentives for risk management programmes tied to Crown Indemnity or liability insurance, whether that insurance is paid by the individual, the hospital or a health-care management authority.

12 A regular cycle of relicensing in seven-year cycles as now required by a number of the American specialty colleges. This should include testing of not only current knowledge but, where appropriate, skills as well. Developments in virtual reality applications to medical education should make this possible.

Elements of this total system have begun to emerge in the British National Health Service and in many health-care systems. At least, they are under discussion. They are the early signs of the future when a comprehensive overall peer evaluation system will become the standard in all our health care systems.

The drama continues, the hidden action becomes clearer and the script improves. The play is endless.

REFERENCES AND NOTES

Foreword

1 Hoffenberg, R. (1987) *Clinical Freedom: the Rock Carling Fellowship 1986*, The Nuffield Provincial Hospitals Trust, p. 89.
2 Ibid., p. 86.

Chapter 1 The issues

1 Shaw, G. B. (1911) *The Doctor's Dilemma*, New York, Brentano's, pp. v–xcii.
2 Freidson, E. (1970) *The Profession of Medicine*, New York, Harper & Row, p. 137; emphasis added.
3 This book accepts the British usage of the word 'doctor' as a generic term for all members of the medical profession, including physicians and surgeons. In the USA, the generic term is 'physician'.
4 Parsons, T. (1951) *The Social System*, New York, Free Press; Parsons, T. (1968) 'Professions' in *International Encyclopedia of the Social Sciences*, 12, London and New York, Macmillan and Free Press, pp. 125–32; Goode, W. (1957) 'Community within a community: the professions', *American Sociological Review*, 25: 902–14.
5 Larson, M. (1976) *The Rise of Professionalism: A Sociological Analysis*, Berkeley and Los Angeles, University of California Press.
6 Starr, P. (1982) *The Social Transformation of American Medicine*, New York, Basic Books.
7 Freidson, E. (1970) *Professional Dominance*, New York, Atherton Press; Freidson, *Profession Of Medicine*; Freidson, E. (1980) *Doctoring Together*, Chicago, University of Chicago Press.
8 Rosenthal, M. M. (1987) *Dealing with Medical Malpractice: The British and Swedish Experience*, Tavistock, London; Stacey, M. (1992) *Regulating British Medicine: The General Medical Council*, Chichester, John Wiley and Sons.

9 Blue Book: *Professional Conduct and Discipline: Fitness to Practise*, London, General Medical Council, (1992), pp. 17 and 22; (1983), p. 15; (1985) p. 16.

10 Rosenthal, op. cit.; Stacey, op. cit.

11 Varlem, C. (1978). 'History of the General Medical Council' PhD thesis, Sociology and Social Policy Department, Bedford College, University of London.

12 Blue Book (1983), p. 15; (1985), p. 16.

13 Blue Book (1989), p. 17.

14 Blue Book (1992), p. 22.

15 Bosk, C. (1982) *Forgive and Remember: Managing Medical Error*, Chicago, University of Chicago Press; Freidson, *Doctoring Together*.

16 Bosk, op. cit., Chs 1–3.

17 Ibid., Ch. 6.

18 Ibid.

19 Ham, C., Dingwall, R., Harris, D. (1988) *Medical Negligence, Compensation, and Accountability*, King's Fund Briefing Paper 6, London, King's Fund.

20 Riegelman, R. K. (1991) *Minimizing Medical Mistakes: The Art of Medical Decision-Making*, Boston, Little, Brown and Co.

21 Bosk, C. (1986) 'Professional responsibility and medical error' in L. Aiken and D. Mechanic (eds), *Applications of Social Science to Clinical Medicine and Health Policy*, New Brunswick, NJ, Rutgers University Press. Fox, R. (1959) *Experiment Perilous: Physicians and Patients Facing the Unknown*, Glencoe, Ill., Free Press.

22 Ibid.

23 Rosenthal, op. cit.

24 Donabedian, A. (1992) 'The role of outcomes in quality assessment and assurance', *Quarterly Review*, 18(11): 356–360; Smith, R. (1991) 'From audit to quality and beyond: a new journal for a critical subject', *British Medical Journal*, 303: 199–200.

25 Klein, R. (1989) *The Politics of the NHS*, London, Longman.

Chapter 2   Making mistakes

1 I first encountered the phrase 'necessary fallibility' in Anderson, R. *et al.* (1989) 'The sensitivity and specificity of clinical diagnostics during five decades: towards an understanding of necessary fallibility', *Journal of the American Medical Association*, March 17: 1610–17.

2 Fox, R. (1959) *Experiment Perilous: Physicians and Patients Facing the Unknown*, Glencoe, Ill., Free Press.

3 Bucher, R., and Stelling, J. (1977) *Becoming Professional*, Beverley Hills, Calif., Sage Publications, p. 23.

4 Bosk , C. (1982) *Forgive and Remember*, Chicago, University of Chicago Press.

5 Light, D. (1980) *Becoming Psychiatrists*, New York, Norton.

6 Bosk, op. cit.
7 Bosk, C. (1986) 'Professional responsibility and medical error' in L. Aiken and D. Mechanic (eds), *Applications of Social Science to Clinical Medicine and Health Policy*, New Brunswick, NJ, Rutgers University Press.
8 Bosk (1982), Ch. 6.

Chapter 3   Friendly efforts

1 Rosenthal, M. M. (1987) *Dealing with Medical Malpractice: The British and Swedish Experience*, London, Tavistock.
2 Department of Health (1992) *Health and Personal Social Service Statistics for England*, London, HMSO.
3 Ibid., pp. 38, 42.
4 Department of Health and Social Security (1961) *Disciplinary Procedures for Hospital and Community Doctors and Dentists* (HC(61) 112), London, DHSS.
5 Smith, R. (1989) 'Profile of the GMC: dealing with sickness and incompetence: success and failure', *British Medical Journal*, 298(6689): 1695–8.
6 Pilowski, L. (1989) 'Mental illness in doctors', *British Medical Journal*, 298(6669): 269–70.
7 Bosk, C. (1982) *Forgive and Remember*, Chicago, University of Chicago Press.
8 Department of Health and Social Security (1990) *Disciplinary Procedures for Hospital and Community Doctors and Dentists* (HC (90) 9), London, DHSS.

Chapter 4   Frustration mounts

1 Bunbury, T. and McGregor, A. (1988) *Disciplining and Dismissing Doctors in the National Health Service*, Keele, Staffs, Mercia Publications, University of Keele.
2 Ibid., p. 22.
3 Department of Health and Social Security (1990) *Disciplinary Procedures for Hospital and Community Doctors and Dentists* HC (90) 9), London, DHSS, replacing the long-standing Circular HC (61) 112 of the same title.
4 Savage, W. (1986) *A Savage Inquiry: Who Controls Childbirth?*, London, Virago.
5 DHSS (1988) *Disciplinary procedures for Hospital and Community Doctors and Dentists. Report of the Joint Working Party*, London, HMSO.
6 'Suspensions: A blot on the NHS', Society of Clinical Psychiatrists Report No. 15, Supplement to the *British Journal of Clinical and Social Psychiatry*, 6(4), Winter 1989.

7 Ibid.: 2.

8 Ibid.: 5–6.

9 Richards, C. (1989) *The Health of Doctors*, King's Fund Project Paper, London, King's Fund.

10 Ibid.

11 Pilowski, L. (1989) 'Mental illness in doctors', *British Medical Journal* 298(6669): 269–70.

12 Richards, op. cit.

13 Rawnsley, K. (1986) 'Sick doctors', *J. Royal Soc. Med.*, August: 440–1.

14 Brooke, D. *et al.* (1991) 'Addiction as an occupational hazard: 144 doctors with drug and alcohol problems', *Brit. J. Addiction*, 86: 1011–16.

15 Ibid.: 1015.

16 Ibid.: 1014.

17 Pilowski, op. cit.

18 Richards, op. cit.

19 Pilowski, op. cit.; Rawnsley, K. (1985) 'Helping the sick doctor: a new service', *British Medical Journal*, March: 922; Rawnsley, K. (1988) 'Sick doctors: measures adopted in Britain and North America to deal with the problem', *J. Royal Soc. Med.*, August: 435–6; Roy, D. (1987) 'How to do it – deal with problem colleagues', *British Medical Journal*, November:1190–2.

20 Pilowski, op. cit.

21 Blue Book (1989): *Professional Conduct and Discipline: Fitness to Practise*, London, GMC; Kilpatrick, Sir Robert (1988) 'Helping the sick doctor: the work of the GMC's health committee', *J. Royal Soc. Med.*, August: 436–7.

22 Smith, R. (1989) 'Profile of the GMC: dealing with sickness and incompetence: success and failure', *British Medical Journal*, 298(6689): 1695–8.

23 Haward, R. A. (1989) 'Doctors requiring rehabilitation following ill health', Report of a Working Party of the Regional Medical Officers.

24 Smith, op. cit.

25 Pilowski, op. cit.

26 Smith, op. cit.

27 Brooke *et al.*, op. cit., 1011.

Chapter 5   Behind closed doors

1 This interpretation was suggested by Dr David Armstrong, Dept. of General Practice, Guy's and St. Thomas's Combined Medical School, London.

2 Freidson, E. (1970) *The Profession of Medicine*, op. cit. Chapter 7.

3 Bosk, C. (1982) *Forgive and Remember*, Chicago, University of Chicago Press, Ch. 7.

4 Freidson, op. cit.

5 Rosenthal, M. M. (1987) *Dealing with Medical Malpractice*, London,

Tavistock; Smith, (1989) op. cit.; Robinson, J. (1992) 'Comments for working party on performance review'. Private correspondence.
6 Freidson, loc. cit. (1970) p.470.

Chapter 6   Empirical research on medical mishaps and mistakes

1 Vincent, C. (1989) 'Research into medical accidents: a case of negligence?', *British Medical Journal*, 299: 1150–53.
2 Report on Confidential Enquiries into Maternal Deaths in England and Wales. (Various report dates since 1952–54). Department of Health and Social Security; Report on Health and Social Subjects: 11 1975, Public Health and Medical Subjects Series #97,103,108,115,119; Cook, R. (1989) 'The role of confidential enquiries in the reduction of maternal mortality and alternatives to this approach', *Int. J. Gynaecol. Obstet.*, 30(1): 41–5.
3 Loc. cit. p. 126.
4 Loc. cit. p. 128
5 Whitfield, A. G. W. (1980) *The Contribution of the Medical Services Study Group of the Royal College of Physicians to Improvement of Care*, London, Royal College of Physicians.
6 Royal College of Physicians (1989) *Medical Audit: A First Report – What, Why and How?*, London, RCP.
7 Donabedian, A. (1988) 'The quality of care: how can it be assessed?', *JAMA*, 260(12): 1743–8.
8 Royal College of General Practitioners (1985) *What Sort of Doctor? Assessing Quality of Care in General Practice*, London, RCGP; Walters, W. and Kelly, J. (1983) 'Attitudes to audit', *JRCGP*, 33: 263–6; Lawrence, M. S. (1981) 'An evaluation of recorded information about preventive measures of 38 practices', *JRCGP*, 31: 615–20; Sheldon, M. G. (1982) *Medical Audit in General Practice*, Occasional Paper 20, London, RCGP; Wilks, J. M. (1980) 'Psychotropic drug prescribing – a self-audit', *JRCGP*, 30: 390–5.
9 CEPOD Steering Group, *National Enquiry into Perioperative Deaths*, London, 1990; Busk, N., Devlin, H. B., and Lunn, J. N. (1992) *The Report of a Confidential Enquiry into Perioperative Deaths*, London, Nuffield Provincial Hospital Trust and the King's Fund.
10 CEPOD Steering Group, op. cit.
11 Busk *et al.*, op. cit.
12 Nixon, S. J. (1992) 'NCEPOD: revisiting perioperative mortality. Same lessons; same problems with compliance', *British Medical Journal*, 304: 1128–9.
13 Bailey, I. S., Karran, S.E. *et al.* (1992) 'Community surveillance of complications after hernia surgery', *British Medical Journal*, 304: 469–71.
14 Ibid.
15 Nixon, op. cit.: 1128.

16 Lunn, J. and Mushin, W. (1982) *Mortality Associated with Anaesthesia*, London, Nuffield Provincial Trust.
17 Ibid.
18 Ibid.
19 Vincent, op. cit.
20 Ibid.
21 Ibid.
22 Gannon, K. (1990) 'Mortality associated with aneasthesia and surgery: a case review study', unpublished manuscript.
23 Ibid.: 9.
24 Ennis, M. and Vincent, C. A. (1990) 'Obstetric accidents, a review of 64 cases', unpublished paper, London, Medical Protection Society.
25 Vincent, C. A., Martin, T. and Ennis, M. (1991) 'Obstetric accidents: the patient's perspective,' *Brit. J. Obstet. Gynaecol.* 98(9): 945–6.
26 Barrett, J. F., Jarvis, G. J. *et al.* (1990) 'Inconsistencies in clinical decisions in obstetrics', *The Lancet*, 336: 549–51.
27 Woodyard, J. (1990) 'Facing up to errors', *Health Service Journal*, 29 March: 468–9.
28 Owen, C. (1991) 'Formal complaints against general practitioners: a study of 1000 cases'. *Brit. J. General Prac.*, 41: 113–15.
29 Neville, R. G. *et al.* (1993) 'National asthma attack audit, 1991–2', *British Medical Journal*, 306: 559–62.
30 Holland, W. (1990) 'Avoidable deaths as a measure of quality', *J. Quality Assurance in Health Care*, 2(3–4): 227–33.
31 Phair, I. C., Barton, D. J. *et al.* (1991) 'Death following trauma: an audit of performance', *Ann. R. Coll. Surg. Engl.*, 73(4): 266–7.
32 World Health Organization, *European Atlas of Avoidable Deaths*. Geneva, WHO (1980; 1990).
33 Shaw, C. D. (1990) 'Perioperative and perinatal death as measures for quality assurance,' *J. Quality Assurance in Health Care*, 2(3–4): 245–51.
34 Barendregt, W. B. *et al.* (1992) 'Autopsy analysis in surgical patients: a basis for clinical audit', *Brit. Jr. Surgery*, 79(12): 1297–9.
35 McKee, M. and Black, N. (1990) 'Does the current use of junior doctors in the United Kingdom affect the qality of medical care?', *Social Science and Medicine*, 3(5): 549–58.
36 Dudley, H. (1990) 'Stress in junior doctors', *British Medical Journal*, 301: 75–6; Godley, F., 'Stress in women doctors: women should not have to overcome more barriers than men', *British Medical Journal*, 301: 16; Firth-Cozens, J. 'Sources of stress in women junior house officers', *British Medical Journal*, 301: 89–91.
37 Dillner, L. (1992) 'Stress in the medical profession: avoidable pressures could relieve doctors' stress', *British Medical Journal*, 304: 1587.
38 Payne, S. D. and Warren, R. A. (1990) 'Patient complaints against an inner city accident and emergency department', *Medico-Legal J.*, 58(3): 153–6.
39 Mihill, C. (1993) 'Cancer errors uncovered', *The Guardian*, 27 August: 1.

40 Salive, M. E. *et al.* (1990) 'Patient outcomes research teams and the agency for health care policy and research,' *Health Services Research*, 25(5): 697–708.

41 Wennberg, J. E. *et al.* (1989) 'Hospital use and mortality among Medicare beneficiaries in Boston and New Haven', *NEJM*, 321: 1168–73.

42 Agency for Health Care Policy and Research (1993) 'Research Activities', No. 166, July, US Department of Health and Human Services.

43 'President's budget proposes $30 million increase for AHCPR', *Health Services Research Reports*, June 1993: 1.

44 Wennberg, J. E. (1991) 'Outcomes research, patient preference and the primary care doctor', *J. Am. Board Fam. Prac.*, 4(5): 327–30; Baraff, L. J. *et al.* (1993) 'Practice guidelines for the management of infants and children 0 to 36 months of age with fever without source', *Ann. Emerg. Med.*, 22(7): 1198–1210; Agency for Health Care Policy and Research, 'New federal guidelines seek to help primary care providers recognize and treat depression', *Hospital and Community Psychiatry*, 44(6): 598; Lee, P. (1993) 'Guidelines: cataract surgery and beyond', *Archives of Ophthalmology*, 111(5): 597–8; Fishbein, H. (1993) 'Patient outcomes research and type II diabetes', *Diabetes Care*, 16(4): 656–7; Weingarten, S. (1992) 'The case for intensive disimination: adoption of practice guidelines in the coronary care unit', *Quality Review Bull.*, 18(12): 413–22; Rochon, P. and Miniker, K.(1993) 'AHCPR guidelines for pressure ulcer prevention: improving practice and a stimulus for research', *J. Geront.*, 48(1): 3–4; Wasson, J. *et al.* (1993) 'The treatment of localized prostate cancer: what are we doing? what do we know? and what should we be doing? The prostate patient outcome research team', *Semin. Urol.*, 11(1): 23–6.

45 Naessens, J. *et al.* (1992) 'Contribution of a measure of disease complexity to prediction of outcomes and charges among hospitalized patients', *Mayo Clinic Proceedings*, 67(12): 1129–33; Huber, K. *et al.* (1992) 'Outcome of noncardiac operations in patients with severe coronary artery disease successfully treated preoperatively with coronary angioplasty', *Mayo Clinic Proceedings*, 67(1): 15–21; Narr, B. *et al.* (1991) 'Preoperative laboratory screening in healthy Mayo patients: cost-effective elimination of tests and unchanged outcomes', *Mayo Clinic Proceedings*, 66(2): 155–9; Sivak, E. and Perez-Trepichio, A. (1990) 'Quality assessment in the medical intensive care unit: evolution of a data model', *Cleveland Clinic Journal of Medicine*, 57(3): 273–9.

46 Berman, L. (1990) 'Evaluation of clinical outcome: a review of government and medical community involvement', *Mayo Clinic Proceedings*, 65: 657–663.

47 Foundation for Health Services Research (1993) *Health Outcomes Research: A Primer*, Washington, DC; Owens, D. and Nease, R. (1993) 'Development of outcome-based practice guidelines: a method

for structuring and synthesizing evidence', *J. Qual. Improvement*, The Joint Commission, 19(7).

48 Farmer, A. (1993) 'Medical practice guidelines: lessons from the United States', *British Medical Journal*, 307: 313–17.

49 Brennen, T. *et al.* (1991). 'Incidence of adverse events and negligence in hospitalized patients: results of the Harvard Medical Practice Study I', *NEJM*, 324: 370–6.

50 Hiatt, H. *et al.* (1989) 'A study of medical injury and medical malpractice', *NEJM*, 321: 480–4.

51 Wu, A. *et al.* (1991) 'Do house officers learn from their mistakes?', *JAMA*, 265(16): 2089–94.

52 Ibid.

53 Anderson, R. *et al.* (1989) 'The sensitivity and specificity of clinical diagnostics during five decades', *JAMA*, March 17: 1610–17.

54 Ibid.: 1615.

55 Ibid.: 1617.

56 Ibid.

57 Landefeld, C. and Goldman, L. (1989) 'The autopsy in clinical medicine', *Mayo Clinic Proceedings*, 64(9): 1185–9; Landefeld, C. *et al.* (1988) 'Diagnostic yield of the autopsy in a university hospital and a community hospital', *NEJM*, 318(19): 1249–54; Landefeld, C. and Goldman, L. (1989) 'The value of autopsy in modern oncology', *Eur. J. Clin. Oncol.*, 25(4): 607–9.

58 McCarthy, B. *et al.* (1993) 'Missed diagnosis of acute myocardial infarction in the emergency room from a multicenter study', *Annals of Emergency Medicine*, 22(3): 579–85.

59 Stocking, C. (1993). 'Echos of error-reflections of response', paper delivered at the 'Expression of Grievance in a Health Care Setting: From Dissatisfaction to Litigation' conference, Centre for Sociolegal Studies, Wolfson College, Oxford.

60 Ibid.

61 Dudley, H. (1974) 'Necessity for surgical audit', *British Medical Journal*, 16: 275–7.

62 Dudley, H. *et al.* (1987) 'Development of a microcomputer-based system for surgical audit and patient administration: a review', *J. Roy. Soc. Med.* 80 (March).

63 Reigelman, R. (1991) *Minimizing Medical Mistakes: The Art of Medical Decision-Making*, Boston, Little, Brown & Co.

Chapter 7   Coming changes

1 Lloyd-Bostick, S. (1994) 'An account model of complaint processes', *Law and Policy*: special issue on grievance in health-care settings.

2 Department of Health (1992) Statistics and Management Information Division, London.

3 Consumers Association (1993) *NHS Complaints Procedures: The Way Forward*, Policy report, London, CA.

4 Ham, C. *et al.* (1988) *Medical Negligence, Compensation and Accountabilty*, King's Fund Briefing Paper No. 6, London, King's Fund.
5 Ibid.
6 Lloyd-Bostick, op. cit.
7 Ibid.: 10.
8 Mulcahy, L. and Jost, T. (1992) 'Dissatisfaction, complaints and legal claims-myths and reality', paper presented at an Oxford–Ohio State conference, 'The expression of grievance in a health care setting: from dissatisfaction to litigation', Wolfson Centre for Sociolegal Studies, Oxford, 4–7 March.
9 Alsop, J. (1990) Interview, 26 March, London; also, with May, A. (1989) *The Emporer's New Clothes: Family Practitioner Committees in the 1980's*, London, King's Fund.
10 Ham, op. cit.
11 Department of Health (1989) *Working for Patients: the Health Service Caring for the 1990's*, summary, London, HMSO.
12 Department of Health and Social Security (1983) *NHS Management Enquiry* (the Griffith Report), DA(83)38, London, DHSS.
13 Department of Health, op. cit., p. 3.
14 Best, G. (1987) *The Future of NHS General Managers: Where Next?*, London, King's Fund; Huntington, J. (1990) 'Changes at the grassroots', *Health Service Journal*, 1 March: 324–5; Taylor, D. (1989) 'Developments in primary care', *Health Services Management*, August: 173–6; Beck, E. J. and Adam, S. A. (1990) *The White Paper and Beyond: One Year On*, Oxford, Oxford University Press.
15 Best, op. cit.
16 Strong, P. and Robinson, J. (1990) *The NHS Under New Management*, Buckingham, Open University Press, 164.
17 Bunbury, T. and MacGregor, A. (1988) *Disciplining and Dismissing Doctors in the National Health Service*, Keele, Staffs, Mercia Publications, University of Keele, p. 12.
18 Department of Health (1989) *Claims of Medical Negligence against NHS Hospitals and Community Doctors and Dentists* (HC (89) 34), London, Department of Health.
19 'Health authorities worried at cost of NHS indemnity plan', *British Medical Journal*, 12 August: 1989: 299.
20 Dyer, C. (1989) 'Defence Societies' Price Wars', *British Medical Journal*, 26 November: 1356.
21 'Health authorities worried . . .', op. cit.
22 West Midlands Regional Health Authority (1989) 'Indemnity of medical and dental staff joint procedural document'.
23 Irvine, D. (1993) 'General practice in the 1990s: a personal view on future developments', *British Journal of General Practice*.
24 Ibid., p. 124.
25 McKee, C. M. (1989) 'Medical audit – a review', *J. Royal Soc. Med.*, August: 474–8.

26 Warden, J. (1988) 'Letter from Westminster', *British Medical Journal*, December: 1429.
27 *Working for Patients*, NHS Review (1989) Working Paper 6 – 'Medical Audit', London, HMSO.
28 Paton, A. (1989) 'NHS Review Working Papers – Medical Audit', *Brit. J. Hosp. Med.*, 41(4): 383.
29 McKee, op. cit.
30 Ibid.
31 Paton, op. cit.
32 Black, N. *et al.* (1989) 'Step by step to audit', *Health Service Journal*, February: 140–1.
33 Weale, F. (1988) 'Audit of a surgical firm by microcomputer', *British Medical Journal*, 296(6630): 1193.
34 'Medical audit – the educational implications', *Standing Committee on Postgraduate Education (SCOPME)*, December 1989.
35 Balfour, T. W. (1989) 'Called to account – a general surgeon', *The Lancet*, 8640: 714–15; McKee, op. cit.; Balfour, op. cit.
36 Paton, op. cit.; Balfour, op. cit.; Axton, J. (1989) 'Called to account – a paediatrician', *The Lancet*, 8639: 662.
37 Dudley, H. (1974) 'Necessity for surgical audit', *British Medical Journal*, 16: 275–7.
38 Godfrey, R. (1989) 'Called to account – a consultant physician', *The Lancet*, 8638: 606–7.
39 Schwenk, D. (1989) 'Medical audit in the UK', *British Medical Journal*, October.
40 Balfour, op. cit.; Axton, op. cit.
41 McKee, op. cit.
42 Anderson, C. M. *et al.* (1988) 'Can audit improve patient care? Effects of studying use of dioxin in general practice', *British Medical Journal*, 299(6641): 113–114.
43 McKee, op. cit.
44 Derry, J. *et al.* (1991) 'Auditing audits: the method of Oxfordshire Medical Audit Advisory Committee', *British Medical Journal*, 303: 1247–9.
45 Lyons, C. and Gumpert, R. (1990) 'Medical audit data: counting is not enough', *British Medical Journal*, 300: 1563–6.
46 Goldman, R. L. (1992) 'The reliability of peer assessments: a literature review' Quality Management Office, VA Central Office, 810 Vermont Avenue, Washington, DC.
47 Horder, J., Bosanquet, N. and Stocking, B. (1992) 'Influencing GPs', unpublished paper. London.
48 Kilpatrick, Sir Robert (1993) 'Rationale behind the GMC's proposed new procedures for the assessment of doctors' performance', *British Journal of General Practice*, January: 2.
49 Robinson, J. op. cit.
50 Kilpatrick, op. cit.

51 Farmer, A. (1993) 'Medical practice guidelines: lessons from the United States', *British Medical Journal*, 307: 316.
52 Hoffenberg, Sir Raymond (1987) *Clinical Freedom*. London: Nuffield Provincial Hospital Trust.
53 Haward, R. A. (1989) 'Doctors requiring rehabilitation following ill health', Report of a Working Party of the Regional Medical Officers.

APPENDIX 1: CATEGORIES OF INTERVIEW CONDUCTED IN ENGLAND, JANUARY–APRIL 1990

At the national level:

Association of Community Health Councils (CHC)
British Medical Association (BMA)
Department of Health (DoH)
Department of Health Regional Medical Officers (DoH RMO)
General Medical Council (GMC)
Medical Defence Union (MDU)
Patient advocates and group
Quality assurance experts
Royal College of General Practitioners (RCGP)
Royal College of Surgeons (RCS)
Social scientists

At the two regional levels:

Chairs of Local Medical Committees (LMC)
Community Health Council Secretaries (CHC)
Consultant physicians
Consultant surgeons
District general managers (DGM)
District Directors of Public Health (DDPH) (formerly District Medical Officers (DMOs)
Family Health Service Authority (FHSA) managers (formerly Family Practitioner Committee (FPC))
Family Health Service Authority members
General practitioners (GP)
Members of Three Wise Men committees (TWM)
Nursing officers (DNO)

Present and former chairs of Medical Staff Committees
Professors of general practice
Professors of general surgery
Readers in general practice
Regional general managers
Regional GP advisers
Regional Directors of Public Health (RDPH), current and retired (formerly Regional Medical Officers (RMOs))
Regional Royal College of Surgeons advisers
Secretaries of Local Medical Committees (LMC)
Unit general managers (UGMs)

APPENDIX 2: ORGANIZATION OF THE NHS IN ENGLAND, 1993

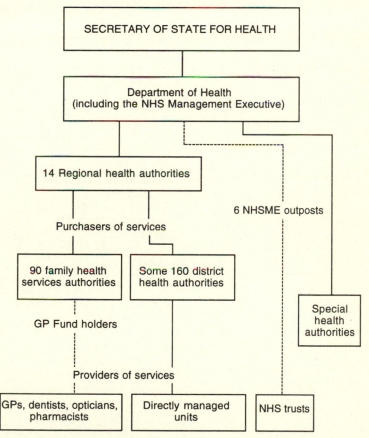

Ham, Chris, ed. *NHS Handbook* (8th edn). Tunbridge Wells, JMH Publishing, 1993

INDEX

FINANCING HEALTH CARE IN THE 1990s

John Appleby

The British National Health Service has embarked on a massive programme of change in the way it provides health care. The financing of the Health Service is at the heart of this change and controversies over this issue are likely to stay with us in the coming decade, whichever political party is in power. This book explores some of the directions that the financing of health care could take over the next ten years. For instance, will the Conservative Government's stated commitment to a health care system financed out of general taxation remain? Or, if the current reforms fail to bring measurable benefits of any significance, will the political pressures to take reforms even further lead to still greater changes in funding, financing and operations? Will the state of the national economy necessitate further reforms? Or might the reforms to date take an uncharted path, with some unexpected outcomes?

For the senior student, academic or health care professional this book offers an expert's view of the financing of the Health Service now and in the future.

> . . . a first recommendation to someone wanting to understand the economics of the reforms and the development of the internal market.
> (*Health Services Management*)

> I believe this book adds significantly to the understanding of health care financing . . . I would add it to the library in any purchasing authority or provider unit.
> (*Health Direct*)

> . . . provides a useful survey of the main issues which have arisen in the debate about the financing of health care in the UK in recent years. It is written in non-technical language, and should be of interest to health service managers and professionals.
> (*Health Bulletin*)

Contents
New directions – Seeds of change – Past trends in health-care funding – The right level of funding – A market for health care – Managing the market: the US experience – Managing the market: the West German experience – Some views of the future – Conclusions – References – Index.

192pp   0 335 09776 6 (Paperback)   0 335 09777 4 (Hardback)

CONTROLLING HEALTH PROFESSIONALS
THE FUTURE OF WORK AND ORGANIZATION IN THE NHS

Stephen Harrison and Christopher Pollitt

For twenty years, British governments of both the left and right have tried to improve the management of the NHS. But the distinctive contribution of the Thatcher governments of the 1980s has defined this very much in terms of controlling health professionals: doctors, nurses and others. This volume

- offers an explanation of why this approach was adopted
- examines in detail the various methods of control employed
- assesses the consequences for the future of professional work and organization in the NHS.

The book will be of interest to a wide range of health professionals, including nurses, doctors, health authority members and managers and will also be useful for students of social policy and health studies.

Contents
Professionals and managers – Finance for health care: supply, demand and rationing – Challenging the professionals – Incorporating the professionals – Changing the environment – The future of managerial and professional work in the NHS – Notes – References – Index.

192pp   0 335 09643 3 (Paperback)   0 335 09644 1 (Hardback)

PUBLIC LAW AND HEALTH ACCOUNTABILITY

Diane Longley

This book examines the relationship between the processes of accountability and management within the health service in the light of the recent
National Health Service and Community Care Act. The author argues that
health care is a social entitlement, to be moulded and allocated according to
rational social choices and to be protected from becoming a commodity
which is largely controlled by unaccountable market forces. Insufficient
attention has been given to the potential role of law in the shaping of health
policy and the management of the health service as a public organization.
The arguments put forward here rest on a firm belief in a constitutional
backcloth for the operation of all government and public services. The
author calls for greater openness in health policy planning, in management
and professional activities, the introduction of standards of conduct in
health service management and for the establishment of an independent
'Institute of Health' to analyse and advise on health policy.

This important and timely book will be of interest to a wide range of
students, academics and professionals interested in health service policy,
politics and management.

Contents

*Diagnostic deficiencies: health policy, public law and public management –
Prescriptive dilemmas: accountability and the statutory and administrative
structure of the NHS – Cuts, sutures and costs: implementing policy and
monitoring standards – Patients and perseverance: grievances and resolution
– Sovereign remedies and preventive medicine: patient choice and markets –
Prognosis and preventive medicine: antidotes, tonics and learning – Bibli-
ography – Index.*

136pp   0 335 09685 9 (Paperback)   0 335 09686 7 (Hardback)

ACY-9358

11/21/95

RA
399
A1
R67
1995